T0339737

Security Operations Center Guidebook

Security Operations Center Guidebook

A Practical Guide for a Successful SOC

Gregory Jarpey

R. Scott McCoy

Butterworth-Heinemann
An imprint of Elsevier
elsevier.com

Butterworth-Heinemann is an imprint of Elsevier
The Boulevard, Langford Lane, Kidlington, Oxford OX5 1GB, United Kingdom
50 Hampshire Street, 5th Floor, Cambridge, MA 02139, United States

Notices

Knowledge and best practice in this field are constantly changing. As new research and experience broaden our understanding, changes in research methods, professional practices, or medical treatment may become necessary.

Practitioners and researchers must always rely on their own experience and knowledge in evaluating and using any information, methods, compounds, or experiments described herein. In using such information or methods they should be mindful of their own safety and the safety of others, including parties for whom they have a professional responsibility.

To the fullest extent of the law, neither the Publisher nor the authors, contributors, or editors, assume any liability for any injury and/or damage to persons or property as a matter of products liability, negligence or otherwise, or from any use or operation of any methods, products, instructions, or ideas contained in the material herein.

British Library Cataloguing-in-Publication Data
A catalogue record for this book is available from the British Library

Library of Congress Cataloging-in-Publication Data
A catalog record for this book is available from the Library of Congress

ISBN: 978-0-12-803657-0

For Information on all Butterworth-Heinemann publications visit our website at https://www.elsevier.com/books-and-journals

  Working together to grow libraries in developing countries

www.elsevier.com • www.bookaid.org

Publisher: Candice Janco
Acquisition Editor: Candice Janco
Editorial Project Manager: Hilary Carr
Senior Project Manager: Priya Kumaraguruparan
Cover Designer: Mark Rogers

Typeset by MPS Limited, Chennai, India

Dedication

For those who supported me through the SOC years; Al Hancock, Linda Merchant, Eric Jones, Larry Doucette, Anna Spychalla, Aaron Burns, Archie Price, Nate Marks, Mike Tillman, Nancy Sorensen, Dale Woolheater and of course my good friend Scott McCoy. Thank you!

For those that inspire me always; my dearest wife Monica, and my precious jewels Jonathan, Aaron & Maija. I love you!

This book is dedicated to my son;

Nicholas Gregory Jarpey

December 19, 1995 – January 28, 2014

A son, a brother and friend to all with a bright smile and quick joke to light up someone's day.

I love you and miss you with all my heart. Rest in peace buddy.

Contents

Part II   Operations

Part III Making the SOC an Integral Part of Your Company

Introduction

This book is intended for anyone who is considering building a security operations center (SOC), already has a SOC, and wants to improve the operations or increase the scope, or simply wants to learn more about what a SOC does and why they are critical to not just the security posture of the organization they support, but when done properly, they also become the hub, which all nonoperational information moves.

Before we dive in, we want to emphasize a point we just made. A SOC is not intended to directly support the day-to-day operations of whatever organization you have. We started this journey at Northern States Power, based in Minneapolis, Minnesota. A few years after we were hired, it became Xcel Energy. As an electric utility, they have an operations center that monitors and controls the flow of electricity across the portion of the grid they support. The SOC has nothing to do with their daily operations, nor should it. For a utility, generating, transmitting, and delivering electricity to customers is their core mission and they do an outstanding job.

The SOC only exists because it supports that core mission. They do this primarily through the monitoring of burglar (burg) or intrusion alarms, fire alarms, panic alarms, camera activity, environmental alarms, card access activity, and anything else that is determined to be important to the operations of the organization. This is accomplished by hiring and training security console operators (SCOs) and giving them clear instructions and solid training and feedback.

Building a world-class SOC is a process. The most important thing to realize going on is that mistakes will be made and things will happen that were never planned for. What is critical to continuous improvement is to focus on fixing the problems and not focusing on the failures.

A ROCKY START

We are both proud of the SOCs we have built and improved, but neither of us started out as experts and the SOC at Xcel Energy had a rough beginning. Initially, we weren't even focused on the SOC. We had a problematic card access system that was costing a lot of money to maintain and had inconsistent performance issues that were hard to troubleshoot. In 1998, it was only a SOC in name. There was a very nice dedicated room with huge custom consoles and monitors lining the walls. The room was built with leftovers from the control center update and it did look impressive at first glance.

It was a one-security offer post, but it was staffed 24/7/365. The primary duties were to monitor intrusion alarms that came through the card access systems and to remotely open gates at a few key facilities when needed. No distinction was made between this and any other post, and the officers on the evening and night shifts were underutilized and often bored. They had been trained to acknowledge alarms and take no further action because of the faulty system. Essentially, guards were posted there to click a mouse.

We'e not going to go through every detail on transformation, but we will say that once we had replaced the card access with a properly functioning system, it became clear that the security officers assigned to the SOC were undertrained and in many cases, over their heads. The next step of attaining an Underwriters Laboratories (UL) certification to monitor fire alarms required that we always have two SCOs on duty, but made us reevaluate what kind of a person we needed to hire.

This book is broken down by chapters in an order we hope makes sense. We start with a needs assessment and move through the business case, construction on to the hiring, training, and development, and end up with chapters on how to take your SOC to the next level.

Developing Your Security Operations Center

CHAPTER 1

What is a Security Operations Center?

While many of you who currently have a security operations center of one kind or another may be tempted to skip ahead, confident that your current incarnation is sufficient for your needs, we encourage you to take additional time and walk through these first chapters and challenge your assumptions. You may, for instance, be convinced that since you already have a facility that you can focus on operations and improvement. From hard experience, we've learned that a business case is not done once approval for a project or function is in place. As your company evolves through acquisition and change in leadership, you will need to justify all that you do and in some cases change those functions to better fit your new environment. In some cases this will require a downsizing, but expansion is also likely. Regardless, the answer can only be discovered if you challenge your assumptions and evaluate the new environment as if you had just taken over the security leadership role.

When you hear the term *security operations center* (SOC), a picture will form in your mind, likely the picture of the first SOC you had experience with or the one you worked with the longest. Like companies, no two SOCs are the same. There are an infinite number of variations, but for our purposes we will focus on the most common delineations.

From an employee perspective, your SOC should be what they think about if they ever think about physical security, just like the help desk is what most employees think about when they have information technology (IT) issues. You aren't just building a room full of stuff; you are building an easily identifiable entity for all things security in your company. Lost a badge? Call the SOC. See something suspicious? Call the SOC. Have something stolen? You get the idea. The phone number should be easy to remember and be located in many different places. Have it printed in the back of your badges or as part of a second card that goes with your badge. Have it located on the home page of your company's internal website. Put stickers on the phones. Whatever it takes to get the word out and whatever works at your company.

3

Security Operations Center Guidebook. DOI: http://dx.doi.org/10.1016/B978-0-12-803657-0.00001-5

It may take a few years to become most people's first thought when a security issue occurs, but be persistent and creative and you will get there.

The first SOC we ever built was at an electric and gas utility. There was a room already built with CCTV monitors, workstations, and alarm receiver, and the server running the card access system. It had one person per shift sitting in it, but this was not a SOC. The room and equipment doesn't make it a SOC, it's the people, processes, procedures, and most importantly, the awareness of its existence. A SOC must be useful to be used, and that takes time in order to build trust and prove competency.

It took a couple of years and a successful business case to get the funding to make that room the SOC that one company needed. By 2007, most employees had no idea that there was a security department other than the SOC. Frankly, they had no reason to know that there was still a group that conducted risk assessments, investigation, and other corporate security tasks. In fact, we prefer to delineate between physical security and corporate security functions. The SOC is firmly in the physical security side, which is basically guards and gates. Corporate security, who the SOC reports to, deals with policy, regulatory compliance, risk assessments, and investigations.

A SOC can be as small as a reception desk that is staffed only during business hours, or it can be a combination of multiple physical locations with dozens of staff working 24/7/365, and in physical or virtual locations all over the globe. It can be staffed by employees and located only on company property, or entirely outsourced. To figure out what you need, at least from a starting point, you will need to complete a needs assessment that is covered in Chapter 2. A large part of that assessment will be figuring out what you want the SOC to do for your company.

Most SOCs have at a minimum, alarm monitoring for the building they reside in and cameras to verify alarms, and verify the identity of employees requesting access at a remote entry and to conduct accident and theft investigations. For companies with one or more locations, the SOC is also a common location to manage the access control system (usually card-based) and often also the location badges are printed. Regardless of the number of locations, centralized control of a card access system and badge printing operation is the most cost-effective. Separating it out and having other groups perform those functions is dramatically more expensive and less secure than centralization, due to the redundancy in personnel and equipment. Speed is always a concern when on-boarding new staff, but even for a large company, photos can be taken at remote locations, printed off hours when the call volumes are down and shipped the next day interoffice or sent via courier. Temporary badges can be used for the few days it takes for the new badge to arrive.

Beyond those more common security-related functions that make sense in combining, there are other less obvious activities a SOC can perform to assist the company and make it more user-friendly or even help the company save money. One option is to be the 24/7 location where all material safety data sheets for the company are located. The SOC number is distributed to all workers and posted throughout the buildings on the safety boards and as part of their site procedures, and if there is an accident dealing with chemicals, employees need only call the SOC to get the instructions read and even sent via smart phone to the appropriate party.

A SOC is a great location to centralize all of the crisis communication for a corporation. Basically, any function when a person can receive a call and take a series of prescribed actions, without the need of making upper management-level decisions (because for many common occurrences, the response can be predetermined), the SOC can follow the procedure and take all of the actions listed. Call trees, documentation, alerting, testing, or whatever. Procedures, training, and documentation are the core strengths of any SOC. One company where we both worked had us take all employee-related vehicle accident reports, because again, they are there 24/7 and the number was selected to be easy to remember, and they advertised in multiple location and formats. For the employee-related car accidents, the safety department had a few thousand key chains made with the phone number of the SOC in the shape of a crashed car, so every company car would have one and everyone would know whom to call. These activities had to be performed by someone, and without a SOC, especially a 24/7 operation, there would be additional expense, usually with some third party who does not understand how your company works or who the proper personnel to contact are.

Once you have decided what type of activities you want the SOC to perform, you need to decide what type of operation you need to support them. We've listed the three most common variations of a SOC: Third Party, Hybrid, and Dedicated. Based on the scope you created, the type of SOC you need should become evident. If not, then you will need to wait until you move onto the business case portion to determine what is the most cost-effective solution that still meets all your requirements.

THIRD PARTY

The configuration and staffing levels of an outsourced SOC are irrelevant, because you only need to focus on two things, the price you pay for the service and whether the outsourced provider meets your service level agreements (SLAs). This may be a good option for a smaller company that can't reasonably fund its own dedicated facility. Likely this type of company also is not a critical infrastructure and may not have many facilities. It is important to clearly define the SLAs to make sure you are getting the services you need in the time and at the quality you require. Contract negotiations are crucial, and if your company is too small to have a robust sourcing or legal department, make sure you get third-party assistance for help in procuring security services.

It's likely that the third party will have some connectivity to your facility if they are to provide access control, monitoring alarms, or viewing cameras, so make sure you have a third party conduct an IT security assessment to ensure that the provider is not introducing additional risk into your environment by having a poorly run IT security program.

HYBRID

A hybrid approach would consist of having dedicated staff for part of the day, but transferring over to a third-party SOC or central station after hours or over weekends and holidays. In some cases, the in-house staff may program access and issue badges, while leaving alarm and video monitoring to someone else outside of normal working hours. Whatever combination, a minimal amount of functionality is required for the in-house staff and it is best to have a dedicated work area for this function. Electronic and physical control of access and monitoring systems must be maintained in the off hours to ensure that there is no abuse or subversion of the systems. This dedicated space has minimal requirements, but if possible, a card reader and camera should be installed to control and monitor access as long as the walls extend from deck to deck, in case there is a need to conduct an investigation. If for whatever reason you can't have deck-to-deck walls, you would also need some form of motion detector inside the SOC to ensure that no one has climbed over the wall to gain access.

DEDICATED

In order to have a dedicated facility, there needs to be a round-the-clock staffing to include weekends, or you are sending your alarms to a third party and fall under the hybrid model. Regardless of whether the staff are employees or contract, someone needs to be on site to monitor the alarms at all times. This is a constant expense referred to by contract security companies as a 168, or 24 hours a day by 7 days a week, including holidays. This can be difficult to staff internally since, unless there is a larger onsite guard force, it will be difficult to staff when people require vacation or sick days. Going to a purely dedicated internal model is a huge step in responsibility and expense for any company and should never be taken lightly. One way to mitigate this is to use contract security staff and require that the post always be staffed in the contract. The contract company will have a larger pool of people to call on to fill the post in those circumstances; however, this will require training multiple backups and putting up with degraded service. The SOC itself may be dedicated and run 24/7 but the staff can all be contract. There are pros and cons to contract an in-house security staff that we will discuss later; for now, we're focused on the facility.

With no reliance from an outside provider, the SOC should, at a minimum, be in a secured location with deck-to-deck walls and have a card reader and camera at the entrance. As with the hybrid option, if deck-to-deck walls can't be installed, some form of motion alarm is required. With dedicated staff on site, it may seem as if these controls were not needed, but with only one person on staff, there will always be some need to leave the SOC for periods of time regardless of how short, be it for bathroom breaks, meals, or to respond to some form of emergency.

This dedicated facility should have an access control workstation and a separate, alarm monitoring equipment, as well as a larger monitor, not only to view the video monitoring system in order to verify alarms but also to assist with granted remote access to a door if workers forget their access card, or to let in contract workers. These enclosed and dedicated facilities, regardless of their size, always seem to have issues with either heating or cooling, or both. There is a lot of equipment located in a small space and most times the SOC is a late addition to an already existing structure. Sufficient outlets are required and they should either be on the building's uninterruptible power supply (UPS) or have their own dedicated UPS on site.

If you decide that you are interested in going with an Underwriters Laboratories (UL) listed facility or for some reason it's required, the cost and logistics will be more than double. Two people must be in the SOC or at least one of them, with the other one nearby enough to be able to return within fifteen minutes. While it's expensive to double staff, there is also a lot of expense in constructing a facility, assuming that the building you want to use even qualifies.

The most common UL certifications are for Burglary, Fire, and Classified monitoring. Whether you already have a SOC or are in the planning stages, UL may not only be viable, but it may help in offsetting the annual expense through cost reduction. For this to be practical, the company would need to have a lot of facilities. At one company, due to the large number of staffed facilities, it made sense to pursue fire alarm monitoring certification, but what we found after a year unto the process is that UL certification has positive unintended consequences. Maintaining certification requires rigorous attention to detail, maintaining paperwork, and well-documented training. The workers also take it more seriously when they realize that lives are in their care.

Once you've decided on the type of SOC that best fits the needs of your company, you will need to outfit it with the right equipment. We aren't going to make recommendations on brands, but instead examine what categories make sense.

An access control system of some kind is likely already in place. If you have multiple locations and also have multiple systems, your goal should be to pick one and convert the mismatched systems onto the standard you've selected. This may not be financial-viable in the short term, but once the systems have exceeded their lifespan, you can replace the old equipment with the new standard. I've known people to try unsuccessfully for five or more years to get enough budget to convert all locations to the same standard and fail to secure funds. If you feel that this is likely with your company, seek instead to upgrade aging equipment a little each year and at the end of those same five years you could have one system. The control panels are essentially ugly computers in a metal case and should be depreciated at five years, making it more viable to replace the equipment over time.

Access control systems include alarm monitoring; however, it is a mistake to assume that you can use it to meet all of your needs without some evaluation. If you have a huge number of additional alarms beyond the associated door contacts, the price point for additional alarm panels may make this cost-prohibitive. In some cases, a simple alarm panel, either stand-alone or integrated with the access control system may be the best solution. Do not rely on the vendor for your design. If you lack the experience in-house to design the system so that it is balanced between your needs and budget, contract with a third party that will not benefit financially from the decision. In a perfect world, large companies should invest in a position that is physical security professional (PSP) certified and sent through card access installation training as well and project management certification. These people do exist, but if you have someone with aptitude, you can get someone up to speed in a year.

There have been a lot of advancements in digital video surveillance and recording in the last decade, but one thing that is unlikely to change in the near future is that IT departments are going to be reluctant to allow bandwidth hogging video to stream across their network without some coordination and possibly begging. Better to include your IT department from the beginning when you are gathering system requirements than to get all the way to deployment and hit a roadblock. In some cases, distributed storage of recordings makes sense with reviewing of video across the network only to conduct an investigation, and in other cases live streaming back to a centralized storage makes the most sense and your network is able to accommodate it. Regardless of which option you choose, consider if or how you will backup the video data. It's likely for insurance reasons if for no other that you will need to rely on the recordings in the case of an accident or theft. If you rely on it, you must ensure that it is backed up in some fashion. When digital video recorder (DVR) units first became available and were reasonably priced, some companies failed to consider this. When a unit went down, most had maintenance agreements in place and the units were swapped out, but the data on the failed units were also lost. With the old tape units, the machine could fail but the video was still retained. Even today, with remote DVR units, this is a situation that is often overlooked until it is too late.

Monitoring technology changes so fast, that the only guidance that will remain relevant for very long is to plan to replace them at least once every three to five years. Make sure that your boss and finance department understands that monitoring screens require replacement and funds should be earmarked every year depending on how many monitoring screens you have.

Each SOC, regardless of size or complexity requires some form of desk or console and chairs. Do not overlook the importance of these items, especially if you are planning a 24/7 operation. Make sure the consoles and chairs are durable and ergonomic. Do not go cheap or you will end up spending even more down the road and disrupting an active operation.

If you do plan on a 24/7 operation, you must also figure out how to accommodate meals for off shifts. Creating a SOC is expensive, so don't cheap out on a couple hundred dollars for a refrigerator, microwave, and large trash can. But you must be forward thinking. Could there be a merger or acquisition that changes the size of your company requiring greater monitoring capabilities? Are there locations that could be added to your enterprise systems? Will your team need to grow and more consoles need to be added? Should the manager or supervisor's office be attached to your SOC? These are questions you must ask now.

In summary, there are as many different variations of what a SOC can be as there are companies. You will need to start with a needs assessment and then choose which option is right for you.

HISTORICAL LESSONS

We didn't start this process as described. Instead, we already had something we called a SOC but really wasn't. We did create a business case for making it a real SOC, but even then, our process was much more ad hoc. When we got to another company, we did follow this process because we were starting from scratch and didn't have the years of experience in the defense sector that we had in the electric and gas sectors. Because of this, we got our SOC up and running and providing valuable services from the first day. We would like you to benefit from our experience and not repeat the much messier growth we experienced at one company. True, we got there in time, but we didn't start with any clearer vision than we wanted it to be better than the one before. Save yourself the pain of lessons learned the hard way and learn from our mistakes.

CHAPTER 2

Needs Assessment

The primary purpose of a SOC is to aid in the protection of assets of a given company. These assets include but are not limited to material, intellectual property, and people. As long as the primary mission is not negatively impacted, the SOC can perform many other tangential and even completely unrelated tasks.

Before we explore what else a SOC can do though, let's first figure out what kind of SOC you need. We will describe a very simple process for listing your needs, and then walk you through the process that we've used in the past.

Here is a big list of all the things a SOC can do. It is not meant to be a complete list, as we can't think of everything, so please add any additional pieces of work that seem relevant. The important thing to remember when you are writing up duties and/or post orders, is that a SCO should be able to follow any written procedure to take action based on a predefined event or activity, but they should not be put in the position of making judgment calls for response to a given threat.

If an intrusion alarm goes off, they must know what is expected. It is perfectly appropriate in the procedure to have the SCOs pull up any camera footage and attempt to verify if an employee set off the alarm inadvertently or if there appears to be an intruder, before calling the police. It is not ok to leave response up to them, and then hold them accountable when you don't like the outcome. On-call investigators or someone in the security management should be working with the SOC and make any judgment calls on behalf of the company.

- Manage the card access system
- Monitor and respond to burglar alarm panels
- Monitor and respond to fire alarm panels
- Monitor heating, ventilation and air conditioning (HVAC) and maintenance alarms
  - Moisture sensor in data center
  - Temperature sensor on refrigerators

11

Security Operations Center Guidebook. DOI: http://dx.doi.org/10.1016/B978-0-12-803657-0.00002-7

- Monitor a variety of alarms through a card access system
  - Forced door
  - Door held open
  - Motion detectors
  - Any other input
- Take incident reports
- Take accident reports
- Take theft reports
- Take in work-order request for facilities
- Manage material data safety sheets
- Key requests
- Program badge access
- Centralized badge printing
- Manage fitness for duty process
- Run access reports for customers
- Test all alarm and access panels daily
- Perform remote security patrols with cameras
- Verify alarm condition with cameras
- Grant remote access via cameras
- Review camera footage for investigative support
- Crisis communications center
- Liaison for guard force
- Law enforcement first point of contact
- Inform IT about network issues at remote sites (the card access panels report network drops and are often the first indication IT could get)
- Call seniority list for union overtime
- Provide overnight monitoring for IT security
- After-hours support for traveling employees needing to report lost company equipment and even personal credit cards.

When conducting your needs assessment, write down everything that you wish to accomplish and be open to coordinating with other departments. Ask other department heads what problems or pain points that they have and what types of duties that they currently pay a third party to perform. Get creative. If something needs to be monitored or if there needs to be a person answering a call or initiating a procedure or even recording an event, the SOC is the perfect place for these activities.

Then write down a description of your company. Is it a single location, or multiple locations? Is it located only on one state or country or is it truly international? Do you own or lease your facilities? Do you currently have a guard force? Are your locations open 24/7? What industry are you in? What regulations govern your company? All of these things will determine not only what you need from your SOC but what kind of SOC you need.

RISK ASSESSMENT

We will describe the different types of facilities and the most common SOC configuration for those companies in the next section. First, we want to strongly suggest that you conduct a third-party risk assessment of your company. There are many reputable companies to choose from and we are not recommending one over another. While you may have many a large team with many certifications, there are benefits to getting an outside perspective.

TYPES OF COMPANIES

Once you have a scope for the type of work you want the SOC to perform, it's necessary to describe what type of company you have. If you are new to the company, this will be an easier exercise since you are biased. If you've been there for many years, it is harder to evaluate your company, but as long as you are aware of that and come at this exercise as if you were an outside consultant, you should get what you need.

We're going to list some basic types of company configurations with examples of the most common security operations we have seen.

A Single Suite in a Larger Office Complex That Operates Primarily During Business Hours

For this type of company, a front desk receptionist or guard with a soft look (not in a traditional guard uniform) is most common. This may not seem like a SOC and it is about as minimal as you can get except for having nothing at all, but because it has such a small footprint, you need to make sure that your roles and responsibilities are clearly defined. You need to ask yourself what you expect this person to do. Does the office complex have its own security? Do you use the building's card access system or do you have your own? Do you need to provide any training to your SOC staff?

Because of the number of small businesses, this may be the most common and also least complicated SOC, but it is also the most often overlooked.

While you may not think of this person as a security professional, they will have some of the same duties. Even if you don't have a card access system, they are working as the access control for your site. At a minimum, you should have a panic button located within easy reach and make sure they know what to do if they are confronted with a hostel guest or customer.

It makes sense for this type of company to have the alarms go to a third party or if the building has its own SOC, for them to go there to be evaluated before the police are called.

A Single Location Dedicated to Only Your Company, with no Other Tenants

It's likely that this type of company will have more employees and more say over the layout. It's also likely that you will have people coming and going outside of regular business hours and may even take deliveries at odd hours. Lobbies and even docks can be set up with two layers of access control and be remotely controlled by either an onsite SOC or a third party. If your company has 24/7 operations and either the facility is located in a high crime area or you have a lot of material that is often targeted for theft, it may make sense that you have a 24/7 onsite SOC with at least one person per shift.

If instead you have an office complex located in an area with low crime and the most expensive assets you own are your computers and office equipment, then it may suffice to have a burglar panel going to a local central station and no onsite security beyond the receptionist described in the example above.

A Single Campus with Multiple Buildings

Multiple buildings could be 3 or 300. Clearly, the number and complexity will determine what is required; however, it is much more likely that an onsite SOC makes more sense in this situation. The more moving parts there are, the greater chance there is for loss and greater likelihood that intruders can access your operations. While third-party offsite monitoring is always an option, dedicated staff, regardless of whether they are employees or contract, have an advantage of being more familiar with your locations. Security is not a passive profession; it is an action verb that requires a proactive approach to be successful. Familiarity helps take this to the next level. The ultimate goal isn't to investigate thefts and determine who is responsible; the ultimate goal is to prevent the theft from occurring.

The nature of the business and the business and the results of the risk assessment will also help determine which approach to use. With the technology currently available, unless the complex is located in the middle of nowhere, it shouldn't matter where within the complex the SOC is located. There is likely network connectivity located in all of the buildings, so there should be no need for expensive trenching or concerns over the distance for panels or card readers because of limitations with twisted shielded pair wire. Should you be in the middle of nowhere or have older buildings that have not been updated with network connectivity to support IP devices, then be careful where you locate your SOC. The place you may want it to be for convenience may end up costing a lot in installation dollars.

Regardless, it is unlikely that this type of company would be able to justify a UL listed SOC. It would take a lot of buildings that are currently being monitored with separate fire and burglar panels going to a third-party central station to justify the expense of the additional second person per shift. The cost of monitoring varies based on a lot of factors, but you should have access to the invoices and be able to tell if you are coming close to being able to offset around $150,000 a year.

Multiple Locations Located in the Same Metro Area

Pricing for monitoring varies a lot based on size and complexity of a building and will also change over time. Let's say for this example that you are paying an average of $1000 a year for fire and $1000 a year for burglar alarms or $2000 per facility on average. We aren't at the business case portion yet, so we are going to list every possible expense. This is a more basic needs assessment exercise to see what approach makes sense for you. If you have 60 locations that means you are spending $120,000 a year on third-party monitoring. Taking on a UL listed SOC starts to make a lot of sense at this point.

With that many locations, your call volume and workload may also justify the additional staff, but that would require you to operate with less staff for at least 6 months and likely more than a year in order to not only get the data you need for a new business case to increase you capacity, but also to wait for the budget calendar to come around so you can spend the funds once it has been approved. This will not only negatively impact retention due to overload, but it also requires you to go to management twice for money within 2 years. It is much better to go to them once with all your data and design the SOC you need from the beginning.

Multiple Locations Spread across a Single Country and Multiple Locations Spread across Several Countries

For your purposes, there is really no difference between these two possibilities. The differentiator has more to do with how many facilities there are versus where they are located. There is still a lot of variation in size and complexity possible, but for the first time, it is likely that you will need more than SOC. The reason for multiple SOC locations is primarily fail over. If you are a critical infrastructure company or the interruption of production for even a single day would cost an unacceptable amount, it may be prudent to have a backup location that has the ability to take over all security operations for a time. This gives you many new options for dividing labor between locations. You could choose to have one location focus on alarm response and the other focus on customer calls and investigative support. Or, your volume may simply be high enough that you require enough capacity that if you had only one SOC you would need at least four people per shift to handle the volume. Even if three are required and the other conditions we mentioned are met, you may want to take advantage of your regional separation and create a second facility. Depending on the type and duration of the emergency, you could bring on temporary staff or possibly even send your more senior SOCs to the other SOC for the duration. If you plan on relying on temporary staff, make sure your written procedures are well organized and easily searchable.

ADDITIONAL CONSIDERATIONS

Your SOC duties may also vary depending on whether or not you own or lease the buildings you occupy. If you lease, you may or may not be directly responsible for fire alarm monitoring, but if you own the facilities, you are definitely responsible and also carry the insurance. If you own the buildings and have several of them, it makes more financial sense to get your SOC UL listed for fire monitoring. Having the same SOC monitoring your fire, burglar, and video surveillance, will have direct cost savings. False intrusion alarms are a common problem. When there is a burglar alarm system that is not connected to a card access system and monitored by a third party, it can end up costing you a lot of money from the local police. Many municipalities charge for responding to false alarms and a few charge a fee even for the first one, but most charge of the site is a nuisance. Having the ability to verify the alarm condition and if there is some problem in wiring or programming, to quickly fix the problem will not only save you from such fines, but it will also ensure that when you have a real break in, that police respond more quickly.

Over time, credibility and even trust are built between a competent SOC and local law enforcement. If you have manufacturing or warehouse locations with material that thieves can easily convert to cash, you want to have build trust with your police department. When they get a call large outfit responding only to a burglar alarm panel with no secondary verification, the response will naturally be slower than when the call come from a person that just rolled the video back 10 minutes and saw a burglar break into the door with a crowbar and can give the police an accurate description, or better yet, send them over a picture captured off the video in near real time.

Since the SOC monitors the same locations every day and has access to the security cameras, they get to know how the location operates. When do most people go home, when the cleaning crew arrives and even who usually works late. This information is then used to adjust the times for when door-held alarms are shunted so they don't become a nuisance and can eliminate the chance of a false alarm even getting to the police.

HISTORICAL LESSONS

Vulnerable Adults

The first SOC either of us ever set up was very minimal compared to prior companies. It was a long-term care facility in Minneapolis about three miles south of downtown. There was no card access and/or only a few poorly placed cameras that were not being recorded. Visitors could come in any entrance without a record. In long-term care, visitors are treated like guests. It makes sense, their loved ones live there and they not only want to feel welcome, they want to come and go as they would if their loved ones still lived in a house or apartment on their own.

Unfortunately, there was also a lot of theft occurring and while it was rare, occasionally a resident would be taken offsite without proper notification. The Long Term Care industry has a small profit margin, and any dollars spent on something like security, has an impact on patient care. These businesses always need medical equipment and facility improvements, so the dollars spent on security must be justified.

After an assessment, we determined to make the front desk, which was already 24/7, our SOC. We changed policy so that only the main entrance was to be used by visitors and even employees after normal business hours. A new card access system was installed with intrusion alarms on all of the perimeters doors. A small video system was also installed with a multiplexor and tape recording system (yes, this was pre-DVR). We got a lot of heat for spending the $100,000 on all of this equipment from the other departments, but we also got lucky. The very first week the new system was in place, we had an elderly woman from the neighborhood attempt to sue our company claiming that she slipped and fell on the ice on our sidewalk just down the street from our main entrance. After checking the video, we saw on the recording that the woman looked around and very carefully laid herself down on the icy patch and then started calling for help.

The company had paid out for this type of accident before and while it's possible those earlier incidents were real, this one was a scam. The next year, we were able to negotiate a lower rate on our insurance that exceeded the cost of the system. The additional benefits were the radical reduction in ambiguity.

We had real access control for the first time and this along with conducting actual investigations for the first time resulted in a reduction in reported theft by 70% and the average loss dropping from $1000 dollars to $100 in the first year. This emphasizes the value of a SOC, but it also points out how critical it is to invest in the tools necessary to support a SOC. The receptionists at the front desk were the same who had always been there. We gave them tools and training and support, but they were the same caring and conscientious people they had been before when they were unable to make an impact. The combination of people, policy, technology, and upper management support is what makes a SOC. Leave any part out, and you will not succeed.

Modest Beginnings

We'd like to say that creating the SOC at one company was all part of a strategic master plan, but the reality is that at first all we wanted to do was to fix our card access problem.

There was a room and it was called the security operation center. There was a wall of monitors that showed the HQ cameras and two remote feeds that refreshed so slowly that if the first frame showed summer, the next would show fall. The card access server sat on the floor under the main console and the second console was dusty and unused. One morning I came in early to see the card access traffic for the first shift in real time to test a theory I had, and I found our lone guard asleep on the floor with the US flag for a pillow.

The guard was let go, but the fact was that none of the guards in that big fancy-looking room had been trained beyond normal guard duties. The alarms came in so frequently that what they had actually trained the guards to do was to effectively click a mouse button to acknowledge everything that came in. The post orders at the main desk covered the SOC and the guards would rotate between the two posts. Occasionally calls would come in during the day, but little security work was actually done.

We were focused on first trying to fix the broken card access systems and then on replacing it. Only when I began to complain about the quality of the officers, did I find out that facilities had tried a few years before when the SOC was first built to gain UL certification. I was told they failed to do so because it wasn't possible. Once we got my business case approved, they replaced the entire card access system that comprised around 40 sites and around 400 card readers (a feat that was also described as impossible) we went about researching the UL requirements. With less than 40 hours of effort and a few hundred dollars for the standard, we discovered it was not only possible, but also relatively easy. That was our second business case and we were able to offset much of the cost by eliminating our spending with third parties for alarm monitoring.

CHAPTER 3

Business Case

Every company has a unique process for creating, reviewing, and approving/denying business cases. The path of creating or improving a SOC is long and challenging. We take for granted that you wish to be successful in the endeavor. If this is true, then in order to have the best chance at success, you must first understand your company. You must understand how it makes money and what it is willing to spend money on. Your best chance at finding this out is to get to know the finance group. Find someone willing to talk about what they do and be prepared to ask good follow-up questions.

It makes sense to take a look at business cases that have succeeded as well as the ones that failed and ask why. Security is a sales job and getting a company to spend money on something that doesn't directly help them make more money will require a convincing sales pitch. The business case, when completed will give you the tools for the pitch, but since it will still be an expense, you may need to build the groundwork ahead of time.

One technique I've used in the past is a customer satisfaction survey. Most companies ask their customers how they are doing, but few internal service providers within those companies do the same. One company required surveys that targeted managers and above on an annual basis and asked a variety of questions. The survey also included a verbatim section so that the employees could list their grievances in detail.

The first year especially, these were hard to read. Security departments aren't always the most popular and people take the opportunity to vent about all the things they are unhappy about from past years. It takes a thick skin to read through them the first time, but what you should see are a few outliers and the rest of the comments falling into a few groups of complaints. A SOC creates better consistency in providing services, so it is very likely that in your business case you can use the creation or improvement of a SOC to directly address almost any customer complaints.

Business cases can span the spectrum from a one-page format to a stack of paper that rivals War and Peace, but they all have three basic sections in

Security Operations Center Guidebook. DOI: http://dx.doi.org/10.1016/B978-0-12-803657-0.00003-9

common. What will it cost, what will it save, and why do we care. The costs should be the easiest to predict. After you complete your specification, you can get hard quotes for construction and material. The labor also should be easy to get solid quotes for. The savings, if there are any, should also be easy to gather. If you will no longer be paying for alarm monitoring from a third party, but you have to give a 90-day notice, you can spell out first year savings compared to future years. Here as with other aspects, spending time to thoroughly research will pay off.

The hardest section is where you list the additional benefits of having or improving your SOC. There are plenty of companies that have gone through this process, so it will benefit you to interview your peers and get their success stories and also their lessons learned. You might even get lucky and find a similar company that has been through this and is willing to share their business case with you.

We have no doubt whatsoever that any company will not only have a higher security posture with a well-run SOC, but that it will also benefit in ways that are hard to predict ahead of time. Companies with a central communication hub like a SOC just run smoother than those that don't. I've described a SOC as the grease that keeps a company running smooth and it isn't an understatement. A well-run SOC sees everything that happens not only at your main facility but also companywide, and it is the pace people can always call to get answers. The SOC may not know the answer right away, but they deal with everyone in the company and can find the answer faster than anywhere else. This doesn't happen over night of course, but it does happen. There is nothing that forbids you from getting testimonials from people in other companies. Don't interview the security director, interview the most satisfied internal customer and ask them why they appreciate their SOC and if they can imagine it going away.

One challenge you will have is that most business cases are designed with the idea that there will be a form of return on investment, or ROI. In the utility industry, capital dollars were cheap because utilities usually own all of their facilities and a lot of real estate, ensuring that they can borrow money at a much lower interest rate the most companies. Since they are also required to gain approval from each state they service to apply for rate cases to determine what they can charge for electricity or gas, operating dollars are always tight. It's because of this that most utilities will approve any business case that saves operating dollars by spending capital funds.

Using very simple math, if you currently have a facility that has a guard on shift 24/7, and the bill rate is $300,000 a year, but you were able to install gates, doors, alarms, cameras, and other sensors to control access and have at least the same or a better chance of detecting a breach with the equipment

Example   21

that you did with a person, then you could propose a business case to replace guards on all but say the day shift. The annual savings for cutting two shifts would be $200,000.

Even companies that borrow money at a higher rate will likely approve of a payoff of three or fewer years with a capital investment, so your capital expense for installation of the new equipment could be as high as $600,000. The utility would often approve paybacks as far out as 5 years, because even with depreciation of the capital assets, the company is guaranteed to save that operating cost of $200,000 a year ever year in perpetuity after the breakeven point.

If you are planning to help justify creating a SOC by reducing the number of guards at remote locations, you will need to ensure that both the equipment at the site as well as the additional dollars is available to cover the building and equipping of the SOC. Again, using simple math at a regular company that requires a 3-year payback, you would have $600,000 in capital per site. Depending on how many sites you could transform, you need to make sure your site costs are less than the $600,000. How much is determined by how many sites you can spread the cost across.

Other potential savings you can add in depend if you are currently paying for monitoring alarms or the additional outsourced services that you could incorporate into your SOC.

EXAMPLE

Once you've listed all of the potential savings, it is important to understand the costs related to running a SOC. These also will be very rough estimates that will need to be verified and all may not apply. If you are going with a third party option, you need only get the quotes. These numbers are related to an onsite SOC to accommodate 2 people per shift 24/7. If you decide you only need or can only afford 1 person per shift, divide these costs in half:

Fixed costs
- Construction of room with deck to deck walls and a man-trap entrance: $100,000
- Workstations: $100,000
- Computers: $20,000
- Large screen monitors: $25,000
- Alarm receivers: $100,000 (if you decide not to monitor alarms beyond through your card access systems, don't include these costs)
- Alarm software: $50,000
- Phone recorder: $50,000
- Other furniture: $25,000

Annual operating costs
- SOC operators: $500,000
- Management: $80,000
- Office supplies: $5000
- Software maintenance: $25,000

Total approximate costs for a fully functional UL listed central station that requires 2 people 24/7/365, is around $1,000,000, $400,000 in capital, and $600,000 in reoccurring annual costs. The labor may seem high, but you will need to pay your SOC operators more than you do for your guard force. This is not an area you want to skimp, as you are relying on their competence for a large part of your security program.

These costs also assume that you already have an access control system and that managing it would simply transfer to the SOC without additional cost. If you have multiple locations and currently have each site print their own badges, you will save money by centralizing to the SOC. In the short run, take at least two, one primary and a backup into the SOC, but as they wear out and need replacing, you will save between $4000−$8000 for the printers per site.

It is possible that you will be able to build a SOC as part of a centralization project that actually saves the company money. For many companies though, there isn't a full ROI. The ROI is not in cash, but in increased security posture and better communication and coordination. If you are in a critical infrastructure or regulated environment, it is likely that you already have a SOC. If not, you will have a greater challenge selling your business case. It is difficult to describe how a well-run SOC positively impacts your company's culture, but it becomes the grease that assists in making operations run more smoothly. I recommend that if you face a challenge, whoever is pushing back, find their counterpart in a company that has had a SOC for at least 5 years and interview them about their experience. Share that data and contact information with your company's counterpart.

At ATK, a defense company, we presented a business case to the controller for instituting a UL 2050 listed SOC that would also centrally manage the enterprise-wide card access system and remotely monitor and review video from several disparate systems. When it was clear that the savings did not take care of all of the expenses, my controller asked me why he should approve it. I had written up all of the additional soft savings and benefits of having a SOC including how our regulatory body, Defense Security Services (DSS) would perceive ATK having a SOC and how it would increase our annual security ratings. I was feeling a little saucy at the time and told him that it didn't matter to me whether he approved it or not. In fact, if he approved it, he would be causing me about a year's worth of sleepless nights

Example   23

until it was up and running and then additional workload for the rest of my tenure. The company would benefit of course, but personally, I would need to work harder and at the same pay rate. He recommended to the CFO that the project be approved. Your mileage may vary.

In this case, the defense company did benefit greatly by having a SOC. A few years later, NISPOM mandated a more comprehensive Counter Intelligence program that requires monitoring workers for aberrant behavior as indicators of potential compromise. The SOC is a perfect solution for this type of monitoring, though some locations needed additional camera coverage.

Make sure to list savings into two categories, hard and soft. Finance usually only cares about hard savings. In reality, it is doubtful you will even reach the level of savings, but instead have what they will categorize as cost deferment. For example, if you spend $300,000 annually in alarm monitoring costs, but the SOC costs $600,000 annually, you will only defray half of the cost of the SOC. Fear not, it is easier to justify spending $300,000 annually than $600,000.

At another company, we already had our UL listed SOC in place and we merged with a company that was slightly larger than ours in employees and number of locations. As often seems the case, the leadership in charge of the merger was from the other company. Their initial reaction was to get rid of the SOC and outsource it as they had with their region. The reality was that in order for a commercial central station to monitor alarms and manage a card access system for a large company, they have to charge enough so that they can make a profit. When we compared the true cost, it was easy for me to convince the leadership that it would be better for us to take over the operations of their company in our SOC and save a few hundred thousand a year while getting better service as an added benefit.

It is our belief that a SOC dedicated to one company, regardless of the status of the workers, will get to know that company and serve it better than a commercial SOC that services multiple companies. If you are a small company, you may need to put up with such an arrangement, but if you are fortune 500 or larger, odds are than a dedicated SOC will not only be cost-effective, but provide superior service to the company.

So now that you have your SOC, you must hope for the best but prepare for the worst and this means already having the business case ready to justify keeping what you already have. Data is your friend. Later in the book we will discuss metrics. Don't skip the chapter or only save it for when you suffer from insomnia. Data is your friend. With it, you can build a compelling business case that will wow your boss, CFO, and CEO. Without it, you may watch years of work slip away, to the detriment of your company. It is ironic that a security department must protect a company even from themselves, but it is your job to do just that. If there is truly a need, then this book can be used as a guide to acquire and improve a SOC for your company, but it can't manufacture the business need. Some companies simply don't need one or while they may benefit, cannot justify the cost for even the lightest version we have described. It may rankle, but the goal of security is to protect the assets of a company. If the loss that a company faces is far less than the solution and the risk to its operations and the potential impact is very low, then less security may in fact be the right call. The obvious extremes are the easiest to manage. It's when you get in the middle and have to weigh the risk to the business and the personal security and safety of the employees that it gets more difficult to come up with the right-sized solution.

Make sure you also keep in the habit of documenting all of the changes that occur in the SOC and what the impacts are, both positive and negative. When things get busy, it is easy to forget, or in a large organization it may be easy to overlook what you consider a small impact. Remember that it is all a part of the whole and needs to be accounted for.

In the fifth year after our SOC became UL listed, we were able to show that through a combination of reduced theft of material, a reduction in insurance costs and by comparing how much it would cost to hire a 3rd party to perform all of the work the SOC performed, that it was dramatically cheaper to keep the SOC than outsource it We proved that it would not only be more expensive, but extremely difficult to uncouple all of the work and farm it out to 3rd parties, and certainly impossible to maintain a 92% customer satisfaction rating while doing it.

Should you already have a SOC but want resources to improve or expand it, then the same advice applies. In fact, you should reevaluate your assumptions every few years to make sure your SOC is still meeting your needs. You should have data that covers not just what volume of work you perform, but how fast and accurately you perform it and how the customers appreciate it. You should have theft trends from before the SOC existed to compare with the trends after it has been in place for a few years. If you don't see a reduction, you need to change then how you are using the SOC.

Since some companies grow through merger and acquisition, there may come a time when you find yourself being taken over by a larger company. Perhaps they also have a SOC and it is better run. Perhaps. It's also just as likely that the security director of that company has never read this book and either has no SOC or has a poorly run operation. Make sure you get your business case to the right people to ensure that your SOC is the one to survive and take over company-wide operations by being prepared ahead of time for the possibility.

HISTORICAL LESSONS

First Attempt

As we stated earlier, the SOC business case was our second. The first business case was to replace the aging card access system.

We had never completed a business case of this magnitude before. The estimate was $1.4 million, based on 400 card readers across 40 locations. That's an oversimplification, because included were also a lot of new equipment, but at that time, in a large project, it was safe to estimate $3500 for an installed card reader. That included new wire, new panels, new card readers, badge printers, card stock, and so on.

But we knew nothing about doing a business case at one company we worked at, and we learned that every company is different. Our boss was the director of security and he let us try but told us we were wasting our time. That it might be possible in 3 or 4 years, but for now, it was a nonstarter. Something about the smug attitude had tweaked us. We decided to find out why it was so impossible.

Our first step was to go to facilities, because they did a lot of capital projects and submitted a few business cases every year. We asked for one that was successful and one that failed. We studied them, but they both looked good. We couldn't tell why one made it and the other didn't, as both pieces of work were essential. We decided to go to finance and ask around. We were soon guided to the team that handled capital projects and luckily that person running it at the time was willing to educate us.

The thing about utilities is that they own a lot of assets, a lot of land, and a lot of power plants and service centers. Since they have so much collateral, they can borrow capital money at a much cheaper rate than most companies. And because they rely on the Public Utility Commissions in each state, they operate to decide how much they can charge for electricity, they are always tight on operating dollars and always looser with capital. While some companies will always lean toward leasing equipment because they are cash strong and asset poor, utilities are happy to lower operating expenses by spending cheap capital dollars.

What that means is that if, say an old and falling-apart card access system was costing around $400,000 a year in service calls and was projected to go up to $650,000 the next fiscal, and the replacement capital expense was

$1.4 million, that the capital project would have a little over a 2-year payback. This company had approved the project with as much as a 5-year payback and a 3-year payback was a slam dunk.

We also found out that capital projects that did not exceed more than one million in a given year did not have to go through the formal proposal process, but rather an abbreviated walk around to get the signatures needed for approval.

We wrote up the proposal to start in June 1999 and conclude in June 2000, with approximately $800,000 the first year to cover badge printers and card stock and the balance of $600,000 to fall in the second year. Like the successful facilities business case, ours was seven pages long and very brief. It listed the why, the how, and the how much in plain speech. Most people that were required to sign did so without looking past the payback page. Only the CFO gave it a good review and stared us down. He asked only one question.

"Do we really need this?"
"Yes sir, we do?"
"Don't go over budget."

The CFO then signed it, smiled, and winked. He knew it was our first and we were very young. In the end, we brought the project in early and slightly under budget, making the payback just a little less than 2 years. The CFO was happy, and we earned a lot of credibility with the executive staff.

Remember, it doesn't end with the approval of a business case. Once approved, you have to do all the stuff you said you were going to do, and hopefully even better than promised.

A Unique Approach

As we stated earlier, every company will have a different process for creating and reviewing business cases and it is likely that there will be different approaches in different business units of the same company. At the defense company we worked at, there seemed to be no documented process for corporate. They had done very few over the years since each location had its own security and facilities staff and budgets. The concept of a corporate-wide initiative seemed like an odd and novel concept to most people we dealt with.

We reused a format from a previous company and put it into a PowerPoint since that seemed to be the preferred method for bringing up anything. It's important to note that one of the reasons we were hired was in fact to build a SOC. My predecessor already suggested it and most people felt like it was a good idea. They hadn't considered the UL 2050 angle that would allow us to monitor our own classified alarms and save some money, so I thought the addition of this data would make it a slam dunk. Instead, I was instructed to present it to our controller, someone who had never been in the loop of all the discussions of how much sense this made and wasn't in the habit of spending capital dollars or increasing the operating budget.

We had not expected the Spanish Inquisition. We were asked point blank, despite having a pile of well-laid-out reasons why it was a good idea (that's what the business case is for), why he should approve this project. Maybe we answered the way we did because we were tired of trying to do what was best for the company, not ourselves, let's be clear, because running a SOC is a lot of work and it can at times be highly political. Maybe it was the attitude in which the question was asked, or maybe we were just sick of the game. Regardless, our answer surprised the controller.

We told him that we were instructed to make the business case and that we sort of hoped it would be denied, since it would take the better part of a year to build and staff it and that afterward it would be an uphill battle to integrate it into the daily workings of the corporation. We were getting paid to do a job without this additional burden and would get paid the same whether it was approved or not.

The look on his face was priceless, but we meant it. Having some form of a SOC is better for any company of size. Certainly, if there are multiple locations or just one really big campus, but it is a lot of work. A lot. Take a picture before, because the creation and integration of a SOC will age you. Once it is up and running, you will be aware of more of what is actually going on in your company and that will require even more work. Of course it's the right thing to do, but we were tired of begging for the opportunity to be overworked.

He approved the funds and we started the journey once again.

CHAPTER 4

Building Your SOC

The first question you may ask when creating a SOC is, "Do I need to build anything?" The fact is, you may not. Clearly if you decide to outsource the entire function, there is no need for a physical space to be built out onsite. Another use case where no construction or remodeling might be needed is if you don't require UL listing as a central station. It's likely that you currently have some form of guard or reception desk and it is possible, depending on what functions your SOC needs to perform, that the existing space is adequate.

If, however, you want to print badges, program access, and/or remotely control other access points through your card access system, then you will likely need a pace that can be locked up when not in use. This could be as simple as building a wall with a sliding glass opening or it may require having a separate room entirely. If your company has multiple locations, assess which one would be best for your SOC. It may turn out that the SOC is not located in the same building as the security department and possibly not even in the same state, especially if UL is required.

When you put forth your business case, you should have already created a detailed scope of work and received at least one bid that covers construction. If you don't require UL listing, you may be able to get away with converting a conference room or office space, but due to the sensitive nature of the room and the work that goes on there, we would still recommend that you modify existing rooms with deck-to-deck walls. A man trap is also a good idea even if it is not required, because eventually, you will need to assist in an employee misconduct investigation and other employees do not need to be poking their heads in the SOC or just overhearing what's happening as they walk by.

If you are curious about going the UL route, then your best bet is contacting the closest UL office and having a talk with the person who inspects UL listed central stations. They will likely tell you to get a copy of their UL Standard 827. Yes, you have to buy it, but if you balk at the cost of the standard, you might not be ready to pursue a UL listing. Read the chapters on Building

Security Operations Center Guidebook. DOI: http://dx.doi.org/10.1016/B978-0-12-803657-0.00004-0

Construction Requirements and Physical Protection carefully to determine if any of your facilities even meet the minimum criteria to be considered as a UL site. The requirements all deal with the fire resistance of the building itself, so it isn't something that can be modified. If the building does qualify, then you must make sure that whoever is performing the construction has a copy of the standard, because it gets down to details like the type of doors that must be used.

One of the biggest stumbling blocks may be the requirement around backup generators and uninterrupted power supply (UPS). You would have to be able to come up with a lot of cost reductions in order to cover these high-priced items if one of your facilities didn't already have them onsite. Don't allow yourself to get bogged down into thinking that a SOC must reside at a corporate headquarters. If you have a location that already has backup generators and UPS, then perhaps that is where the SOC should be located. Communication between a SOC and the rest of the company isn't done in person, but by phone and email, so the SOC can be located anywhere.

One of the things that the standard doesn't talk about that we learned the hard way was the need to additional air conditioning and even heat in the winter. Having deck-to-deck walls can put a cramp on any central air system, but even a normal amount of cooling may not overcome the additional computers and monitors that fill up the usually small space. Depending on where in the building the room is, the opposite problem could occur in northern climates and even all the additional equipment may not generate enough heat to make up for the loss of circulated air caused by the new construction. Make sure to include facilities in your planning stage and take the heating/cooling into account.

When designing the size of your SOC, try to plan for future growth. You may think you will only ever need two workstations, but things change and it's cost prohibitive to move a SOC and should only be done so when you have no other choice. Also, if the budget allows, design it with a raised floor like a data center. It will make your initial installation much easy and future repairs and changes much less painful. Don't skimp on the moisture sensors.

Once you have the building requirements met and the facility constructed, you will need to make sure that you follow UL 827, which sets standards for the required hardware and communication systems. Everything in UL is very precise and each type of item used for monitoring of alarms such as fire or burglar needs to meet their own UL standards, and redundancy is the key. Not only will you need to have two of everything, but your SOC operators will be required to routinely train on how to switch from the main to the backup. This will require some preplanning to be included in your design, since they will need to get to the back of the alarm receivers. Color coding and clear labeling will make it easier.

It may seem like UL is difficult and confusing and it can feel that way when you start because you are learning the process. We don't get any pay or other forms of compensation from UL. Having said that, make sure to have your plans reviewed by your UL inspector before you begin any construction. It would also help to reach out to others in the security industry and through members of your local American Society of Industrial Security chapter at a monthly meeting. The UL folks are not your enemies. It is not a confrontational relationship. Your SOC will have the responsibility of calling fire or police for emergency situations. The lives of those your site monitors will be your responsibility. Because of this, the UL inspectors take their jobs seriously, but that means they also are extremely helpful. Their goal isn't to prohibit you from monitoring alarms, but to assist you in monitoring in a safe and reliable way. You will need to pay for their time and expertise through an annual fee, but they are not there to get rich from consulting and even if their process weren't reasonable, they would be worth it. Ultimately, UL certification will force your SOC to be the best at their job by ensuring you are covering the basic needs of staying in production and working no matter what the outage.

WORKSTATIONS

There are very few companies that make workstations for this type of function. We've played with a couple of different designs over time and one thing that became clear was that the more room available for desk top space and storage, the better.

Chairs are also often overlooked. Do not go cheap. With all the press about sitting being the new smoking, you may even want to consider installing standing workstations as an option. Sooner or later, though, someone will need to sit and the chair should be part of the overall ergonomic design. Also, remember that the phones, computers, and chairs will all be used 14/7/365 and by multiple people per day. Make sure to have cleaning supplies available and required people to clean their workstations before starting their shifts. Also, since the equipment is getting used three times more often and by a variety of bodies, make sure to budget for replacements accordingly. If a chair normally lasts 3 years, get new chairs annually.

While not compulsory, video monitors are a common component of most SOCs. Luckily the price keeps going down and frankly, there is no need for the latest or greatest resolution or features. There are different grades of monitor out there. When pursuing options, request commercial models for your specifications. They are designed to be left on continuously for a few years, and that's what is needed. When it comes to computer equipment, the same thing is true. Order your equipment from places that support call centers. We also believe strongly in overbuilding everything and that includes computers. Replacement of equipment is expensive and if budgets get tight, it's often the first thing to be cut. Make sure you get the most powerful processor, the most RAM, and the largest hard drive as you may be stuck with this equipment for a while.

A few other nice-to-have items are dry erase boards, bookcases, a refrigerator, and a microwave. If possible, install a bathroom inside the SOC. With a small kitchenette and a bathroom, you will be truly self-sufficient. Of all the things I just listed, the bookcase may have caused an eyebrow to be raised. After all, everything is online today. If it isn't in some application running on the corporate network, it can be found online. Why would you need paper? You will definitely need file cabinets to hold all of your UL required reports and maintenance documents, but a hard copy of all of your post orders and procedures is a good idea. Network outages and distributed denial of service (DDOS) attacks occur, so even if you have your UPS and backup generators, it's possible for your network to be down and for you to lose access to the Internet. If your land lines, cell phones, and local band radios are also out, then no amount of books will help you. Just go home and be with your family. Short of that though is a level of degraded operation where you will be glad you have all of the phone numbers and procedures available on paper in well-organized binders.

HISTORICAL LESSONS

This is not a smooth journey. Like any project, there will be problems along the way. Make sure that you build in both contingency time and money. Take a hard look at all of your assumptions and then plan on some of them being wrong. When we started our journey, we knew all this and planned for it. What we didn't plan on was that every time we had UL inspect our SOC, especially the first time, we would get conditional approval and a long punch list of items to correct. It was unlike any process we had been through before. Some of those items were merely clerical or training changes, but some required money.

If you are not pursuing a UL listing, you won't escape this process completely, because creating something new always comes with expectations, some of which are not vocalized until it is real. You may have communicated well up the chain throughout the entire process, but at some point, someone will come to you, usually just when you think you are done and say, "What about X?".

Perhaps X is an unspoken expectation of a reduction in theft, or perhaps there was an assumption that your SOC staff could also perform other tasks that require them to leave the SOC unstaffed for a time each night.

Regardless of what it is and where it comes from, do your best to reset expectations while meeting your new requirements. Hopefully, you will not have that many Xs and the ones you have will not be expensive to implement.

At one company, upper management assumed that our number of incidents would decrease. Over time they did, but initially, they increased because we finally had one place to report them all. The online reporting form also helped as did our security awareness training, but for the first time we felt we were getting close to the real number of incidents being reported. That bump in numbers was obvious to us, but management was surprised and that is never a good thing. When we worked together at another company, we made sure to warn management that we would see a bump and why.

CHAPTER 5

Staffing Options

There are two basic kinds of staffing model, contract or in-house. With those two you can have a wide variety of combinations. You can have all in-house, all contract, or a mix. You can also, if you convince a vendor to agree, have contract to hire.

Day time SOC in the only building it supports.

Day time only SOC with only a few other buildings to support.

Day time only SOC with many locations that it supports.

24/7/365 SOC located in the only building it supports.

24/7/365 SOC supporting many locations.

24/7/365 UL listed SOC.

Of course, if your SOC is completely outsourced by an offsite vendor, then staffing is not your problem. If, however, you have one of the options listed above, you will need to decide how to staff it. There really is no right or wrong answer.

Proprietary staff are likely to have better benefits and better pay that contract. Because of this, they usually have lower turnover. This is not an imputable fact. Proprietary staff could be paid poorly and treated worse, causing a higher rate of turnover than the average contract company suffers.

Here are some pros and cons:

Proprietary SOC operators

- Usually cost more (con)
- Less turnover (pro)
- When turnover occurs, overtime can be costly (con)
- Hard to staff anything more complicated than a straight 40 (con)
- Hard to cover vacation and cover breaks (con)
- You directly supervise the workers (pro and con)

35

Security Operations Center Guidebook. DOI: http://dx.doi.org/10.1016/B978-0-12-803657-0.00005-2

- You are directly involved in the hiring and firing (pro and con)
    Contract SOC operators
- Usually cost less (pro)
- More turnover (con)
- When turnover occurs, there is no cost impact (pro)
- Staffing any shift is the responsibility of the contractor and guaranteed (pro)
- Vacation and breaks are handled by the contractor and coverage is not effected (pro)
- You don't directly supervise the staff (pro and con)
- You are not involved in the hiring (pro and con)
- When you are unhappy with the performance of a worker, you simply have them removed from the contract. You do not have the ability to fire a contract worker, nor do you have to deal with any of the related issues (pro).

This is a topic that has been covered many different times in many different ways and will likely be a topic of conversation and debate for years to come.

When making the decision, you need to be honest about what your or your company's goals are in relation to staffing a SOC. As the security practitioner, it is your responsibility to make sure all parties involved understand the consequences of those goals and influence the outcome.

A SOC post is different than work that is traditionally seen as a guard post. The duties are more numerous and complicated, requiring a higher caliber of worker who is able to, within the confines of post order and procedures, use sound judgment. While prior SOC experience is not crucial if you have a good training program in place, it is desirable and you will either pay more for it or not get it. SOCs are more prevalent now than they were even 10 years ago, so solid salary data exists for each major market.

Before making the decision on which path to go down, you should benchmark companies in your area to determine whether they primarily use contract or proprietary and if possible, find out what the going rates are for both.

Proprietary is an industry term used to described security officers who work directly for a company. It is a way to differentiate them from contract workers who may work in your facility, but work for a company that is licensed to provide guard services.

These employee security professionals are traditionally paid on an hourly basis. The pay range varies by what type of duties they perform and under what conditions, but it is common for proprietary security professionals to get paid slightly more than their contracted counterparts. Since they are employees, they usually also get better benefits.

The pros to using proprietary workers are that based on metrics for the last few decades. The turnover for employees in these roles is less than that of contract workers, likely due to the difference in pay and benefits we mentioned. Other pros would be being able to supervise them directly.

Contract workers as described above, work for contract guard companies. Contracts traditionally last 3−5 years. Changing the number and type of positions under the contract is not uncommon and as with all contracts, flexibility is determined by the language in the agreement and the relationship between companies.

The pros of using contract workers deals mostly with shifting the burden of filling shifts from the employer to the contract company.

The reason why there are very few proprietary guard forces still in existence is that most companies weighed the pros and cons and determined that contract made the most sense. The costs are predictable, the burden falls on the contract companies and they have specialized in recruiting and retaining security workers. But if you decide to use a contract company, that does not mean that you must settle for all of the cons listed. The biggest con is turnover. This may be less serious for many guard posts, but for CSOs, knowing the company, systems, and people takes time and is more than a benefit, it's a requirement for top performance.

A coworker told me many years ago that you can tell a contract company what the hourly rate for the guards will be or what the bill rate you are willing to pay, but not both. A contract company must cover all of their overhead and profit margins in the percentage difference between those two numbers. While everyone wants a fare deal, you can't expect a contract labor company to work without making a profit. Never, ever begrudge a company a fair profit. That doesn't mean you shouldn't question what is in a bill rate. We recommend actually quite the opposite. The profit margin also doesn't need to be a secret. You have a fiduciary responsibility to make sure that you are getting the best deal you can for your goods and services. In your Request for Proposal, make it clear you want to see a detailed breakdown of what makes up the bill rate.

If you've done your research and know what the going rate for a CSO is in your market, then you need to make sure the hourly rate is at least equal to that going rate. The contract company will likely be on top of this as SOCs are more common and contract companies have more experience with them, but it doesn't hurt to reinforce the importance of keeping the SOC staffed with qualified operators at all times.

Since the contract company that wins your business will likely be competing with a few other companies, once the bid has been awarded, you should have a talk with the management of the contract company about your expectations. If your number one reason for selection was the low cost and you begin to see higher than expected turn over with no other obvious cause, then you are as much to blame as the contract company.

Let's assume that you ensure the CSOs are getting a fair pay rate and you still have turnover issues. One way to stabilize the turnover is to offer something more. Perhaps it is 50 cents more than everyone else in your city. Perhaps it is a better health benefit option or the number of vacation days. Regardless, the decision to add this benefit will impact your bottom line and you need to plan for it. The best time is from the beginning of a contract. Budgets are always tight, but if you are already spending, say $700,000, on contract labor and are unhappy with the results, don't hesitate to spend another $20,000 to get the results you want.

TRAINING

Regardless of the employee type, if you want more stability, which equates to less turnover, you need to pay at least as good as everyone else in your area and offer something that competitors don't. Let's face it, a company down the street in a different industry is still a competitor for talent. Training is a differentiator. It also serves two purposes. Getting better performance from the workers you have and showing those workers that you value them enough to invest in them. If you handle it right, you can get some training for free. Buy a big new card access system and negotiate extra hours of training. Increase the customers experience by giving customer service training, possibly from your own customer call center.

CAREER PROGRESSION

One of the differentiators you can have for improved retention beyond pay, is a chance to move up the ranks, which is not always available for security officers at many job locations. We had many security guard positions that we could draw from, by identifying the sharpest and hardest working guards and then by providing them with cross training so they could fill in at the SOC over holidays and vacations and when we had turnover. When a SOC position became available, they still had to apply, but we already knew if they would do well because we had been able to observe them in action as a security officer and a SCO. The SOC pay was around $3−5 more an hour, which is a big deal to someone whose base pay is probably between $10 and $15 an hour. Then we had two levels of operators with clearly stated requirements. Having a senior operator position (one per each shift) gave the operators something to strive for. Finally, we had salaried employee positions titled Security Systems Consultants. They were required to have or within the first year attain the PSP certification from ASIS International and worked with the vendors to install security systems and manage the key system in their region. We gave preference to SOC operators whenever these roles opened because they provide a form of career advancement. During the time we were in that company, we saw a couple of guards rise all the way though the SOC and into those Security System Consultant roles. Having a career path within a contract is unheard of, and that is sad. It isn't just the contract company's job to think about these issues, but should be a partnership.

RETENTION

We broach the subject, but we can't stress this enough. Hiring is a difficult and irritating process that does not always result in success. We both lived through a nightmare years ago when we had a contract worker act professionally throughout their probation period of 3 months, only to morph overnight into the worst worker ever in that SOC's history. That is an extreme and unique case. It's more likely that at the end of a trouble-free probation, you will have a good addition to your SOC. Once you have them, keep them. It is so much cheaper and easier to retain good workers than understand your operation than it is to search for new people. In order to do this, you need to have clear expectations, ask them for feedback, act on feedback if only to respond to a concern, pay them a fair wage, give them a benefit that is a true differentiator that they care about, and last but not least, treat them with respect. Contract workers are often treated as second-class workers. This needs to stop. Your company relies on every contract worker to perform a function that costs time and money. Why would you then antagonize those same people?

By providing a respectful work environment, offering a fair wage, and providing a few additional benefits as well as career progression path, our turnover rate was less than 15% annually. If you've benchmarked guard force turnover, you know it is commonly between 70 and 90% annually. Our rate was unmatched and frankly the money we spent on a slightly higher wage and a few other small additions were worth tenfold what we got in return on stability and quality.

HISTORICAL LESSONS

When we built the SOC at one company, we already had a contract guard force. All the guards were paid the same wage and there was not a standard for SCOs. We knew they needed more, but there wasn't a huge amount of market data to choose from. At first we were only able to give them about a dollar more than regular guards, but over time we were able to add more and even differentiate between junior and senior SCOs.

That certainly help our retention, but we knew we needed to do more than that. We put in change orders to offer insurance. We also added in time for real training and a slightly reduced pay scale for a 1-month indoctrination program. By paying more and having two levels, as well as providing a better quality of work environment, we were able to take talent from other downtown operations. Eventually, we needed to replace card access systems in both Colorado and Texas after the merger. Instead of searching for what at that time didn't exist, essentially what a PSP-certified security professional is today, we recruited from the SOC and found an excellent candidate who knew our system, had shown a lot of promise, and was willing to relocate. Eventually, we had a permanent position in each of our three regions and two of the people had come from the SOC.

With upward mobility an actual reality, we could assist our contract guard service in hiring and retaining higher quality talent. If you take the position that all of that is the responsibility of the guard company and you need not concern yourself, then you will have to live with quality issues as a result of high turnover. While most contacts had upward of a 100% turnover annually, ours was less than 20%, with the SOC being less than 10% annually. The consistency that we gained was worth the relatively small incremental increase in cost for salary and minimal benefits and the additional levels, from hourly to salary positions did even more to recruit and retain top talent.

Operations

CHAPTER 6

Responsibilities and Duties

INTRODUCTION

In this chapter, we write about the responsibility of presenting to your SOC staff the importance of their duties when they arrive for their first day of work. This will include your mission statement, an introduction to their role as a SCO, and why their job is important.

We will provide a template SCO job description: staffing schedule, discuss their supervisory authority, and summarize the responsibility of the SOC staff. We will cover the basic duties you need to determine what they will do and discuss what they can do. For the sake of this writing, going forward, we will assume that your SOC is UL certified and requires two SCOs per shift.

What does a security officer do? That answer can be summed up easily in three words "observe and report." What does a SOC operator do? That question is answered as easily as the first question with the addition of one word, "observe, communicate and report." When planning your organization's responsibilities for your SOC, it is crucial to create your SOC operator procedures with the idea in mind that your operators are not there to make command decisions. They are there to observe alarms, observe video, communicate with both the internal and external customer and report that information back to the chain-of-command or other designated individuals such as facility managers, safety managers, or site security managers of any area as specified in the post orders.

WELCOME TO THE SOC—YOU HAVE AN IMPORTANT ROLE

When starting a new SCO, you must ensure that they understand their role in the security of your organization, which is important to the entire team. They must know their role and the great responsibility that it carries. Their company depends on them to protect their property from burglary, fire, and many other dangers and threats. You need to have a dedicated training program, with a training checklist and updated post orders and site procedures,

Security Operations Center Guidebook. DOI: http://dx.doi.org/10.1016/B978-0-12-803657-0.00006-4

which they will utilize to perform their regular duties and daily tasks. Training will be covered in Chapter 8, Training Program.

Through diligent reading of the procedures and understanding of the software and equipment they use, they will be able to do their job. SOC leaders must make sure the SCOs understand that if they do not know how to do something or need additional training that they bring it to their supervisor's attention immediately. That is the only way they and the team will continue to learn and get better at their job. No SCO should ever be made to feel bad about asking questions when they do not understand one of the tasks they are supposed to perform.

Through the monitoring of burglar, fire, panic, or HVAC alarms and camera systems, they become the eyes and ears of the company. Their alertness and ability to thoroughly perform their duties can help prevent the loss of life and damage to company property with a quick alarm response or observation of illegal activity on a camera.

MISSION STATEMENT

Mission statements are used to communicate the purpose of a team, department, or entire organization. Your SOC, if it is properly integrated into and utilized by your company, should touch the entire business organization. Create a SOC mission statement and hang it on the wall in an area where the SCOs can see it every day when they report for their shift, so they are reminded what their mission is on a regular basis. Create this mission statement to reflect your company's business mission statement and core values. It should be a simple one-page statement that can easily be read quickly and highlights the most important goals the SOC is supposed to uphold. The vision and mission for your SOC are the two most important factors that should be written on your statement. Professionalism, customer service, and dedication should always be stressed. If you have room available for it on your mission statement, write a short list of services that the SOC provides to the entire company.

SCO JOB DESCRIPTION

This is one of the hardest tasks of creating a solid SOC team. When you have two people working side by side in the same room for 8—12 hours a shift, they need to be able to get along at least on a professional level. They do not have to like each other, but if they are professional, they should be able to perform their duties and communicate with each other as professionals to accomplish the mission. All it takes is one sad sack energy vampire to suck the motivation out of the rest of the staff. The person who cannot carry their own weight and relies on their team members to help them through a shift, or the repeat offender who calls off shift if he or she stubs their toe will begin to drain the life right out of the entire team. "Why should I work hard when they don't?" That will become the question and as a manager or supervisor you must not allow that to continue.

The SOC needs employees who understand the role of security for an organization. They must be able to communicate both verbally and in writing with people on a professional level. They should have the computer skills to monitor alarms, perform programming of physical access control system, document in an electronic daily activity report, email internal and external customers, and write quality incident reports that can be used in a court of law. To be considered for hiring, SCOs should have experience in at least two of those three very important categories: security experience, customer service experience, and computer skills. Previous central station alarm monitoring experience could be equal to previous security and customer experience. Security experience could include working as a security officer, law enforcement officer, any prior military experience or even a receptionist where security was stressed by documenting all visitors and reporting security incidents. Customer service experience should include any type of experience in communicating with people on a regular and daily basis such as working in retail, fast food, or any job that has you interacting with customers on a regular basis. Security and customer service can be taught but basic computer skills are a must. It is better for the whole team if you don't have to train them in both security and customer service. The new hire candidate must be able to handle the basics of email, documents such as Microsoft Word or Excel and various software packages for access control, various alarm monitoring, and camera systems that are in your SOC. There are other factors depending on your business that could be crucial to hiring such as the need for the applicant to acquire a security clearance with the Department of Defense (DoD) or the Department of Energy (DoE).

Leadership experience is also a plus and that will be discussed more in supervisory authority related to larger companies. When hiring, do not be afraid to hire potential leaders for the future. They often become peer leaders within the team and when the opportunity presents itself they will be ready and eager to step into a leadership role.

SAMPLE SCO JOB DESCRIPTION

The following SCO job description can be used as a template for your SOC. Tailor it to fit your needs within your organization.

JOB TITLE: Security Console Operator (SCO) All Shifts
LOCATION: Security Operations Center (SOC) at XYZ Location

Position Summary

The SCO is responsible for processing fire/mechanical/panic/intrusion alarms and video monitoring systems, to include basic programming of each system, performing basic clerical duties to include data entry and filing. SCO will provide outstanding customer service and satisfaction by handling customer inquiries and concerns regarding security incidents, alarms, site and personnel changes, system and equipment problems, and other questions/notifications regarding service provided by the SOC through various forms of communications. SCO shall adhere to all post order standards and follow policies and procedures set by the company. SCO shall follow up with information and research regarding assigned projects, events, and requested services accurately and in a timely manner. The SOC is a 24 hour/365 days a year operation with a minimum of two SCOs working each shift on a rotation schedule.

Duties and Responsibilities

- Successful completion of New Hire and SCO Level 1 and 2 training programs.
- Successful completion of mandatory On the Job Training (OJT), Continuing Education Program (CEP), and UL monthly training requirements.
- Monitor and maintain the fire, card access, intrusion, mechanical, and panic alarms systems while responding accordingly and professionally in a timely manner.
- Monitor various site camera systems and conduct after-hours site tours using video surveillance.
- Perform system checks on equipment and software applications, recognize and correct minor problems, and accurately report concerns and problems with equipment to customers, business partners, vendors, corporate security personnel and/or SOC management.
- Record pertinent information from site/field personnel and enter accurately into reports and in a timely manner notify the appropriate personnel.
- Solicit pertinent information from potentially emotional callers and relay complex facts and details accurately and concisely to the appropriate personnel.
- Prepare, complete, and process necessary reports to include SCO stats, work orders, daily activity, and incident and condition reports.
- Monitor and maintain all forms of communication to include email, phones, cell phones, hand-held radios, pagers, fax machine, and/or personal contact with customer while responding accordingly and professionally in a timely manner.
- Act as liaison between various law enforcement and government entities.

- Act as after-hours supervisor for all field security officers in the absence of other management.
- Assist the SCO supervisor with required shift coverage to meet daily contractual requirements and activity.
- Perform other duties as assigned by the client and/or management personnel.

Qualifications

- High school education or equivalent. Two-year degree or higher preferred.
- Minimum of 2 years' customer service, central station monitoring, and/or security experience, or an approved combination of all three.
- Strong teamwork and communication skills. Must be flexible/adaptable to a constantly changing environment.
- Ability to make verbal and written presentations relating to SOC operation.
- Intermediate to advanced level keyboard and computer skills.
- Ability to coordinate multiple assignments, actions, and direct others to locations and tasks.
- Ability to use sound judgment in stressful situations and capable of staying alert during periods of inactivity.
- Ability to work without close supervision.
- Ability to keep privileged information confidential.

Physical Demands/Environmental Conditions

- Works primarily in a climate-controlled office environment that is often cooler than normal to keep computer equipment cool.
- Ability to perform finger and hand manipulation and performing repetitive motions to use office and various security equipment.
- Ability to exert up to 10 lbs. of force when moving items such as computer printout paper, notebook ledgers, office equipment, and so on.

HIRING AND INTERVIEWING YOUR SCO CANDIDATE

Background checks are a must and we will assume that your company conducts a background check on any potential new hire. When bringing the candidate in for an interview, start off with a tour of the SOC, so they see what type of environment they would be working in. Describe to the applicant the various SOC duties that are required, the hours they would be working, what a typical shift is, and what an extremely difficult shift could be. You should accentuate the fact that during a shift it could be very quiet and boring one second, and then become extremely busy with alarms and phone calls happening all at once. This allows the applicant to see firsthand that the ability to multitask is something that is crucial to the success of your SOC and should be asked about when interviewing a candidate. Each company is different and may have their own required questions to ask for any position. We have provided a short list of questions that we have found to be helpful when conducting interviews with SOC applicants. Be sure to document their answers carefully for your review later.

SAMPLE INTERVIEW QUESTIONS FOR A SCO

Tell us about what you are currently doing and/or have done in the past for employment?

What was it about the SCO position that interested you?

What do/did you like most about your current/last position?

What do/did you like least about your current/last position?

Tell us about a time you had to deal with extreme adversity with another person, how did you handle it and what did you do?

Tell us about a time that you do not get along with a coworker. What was the problem, and how did you handle it? Were you able to resolve the problem?

Please describe what you believe it is to be "professional?"

What is your greatest strength?

What is your greatest weakness?

Getting the job done involves gathering information and input from others. How do you do this?

Please describe your computer experience and abilities?

What operating systems are you familiar with?

Are you familiar with MS Office suite (or whatever your company uses)?

How would you rate your knowledge of that software?

What security-related software systems are you familiar with such as access control, alarm monitoring, and video surveillance? How would you rate knowledge of these systems?

Please describe your customer service experience and abilities?

Please describe what you believe to be good customer service?

In your opinion, how does customer service relate to the security industry?

What have you done that shows initiative and a willingness to work?

When short-term projects clash with long-term ones, which one takes priority and why?

How would your supervisor get the best out of you?

How do you establish a working relationship with new coworkers?

What are your long-range goals?

What is your idea of the best job you could have and what would you do there?

Tell us why you're the best candidate for this position?

Anything else to add?

Questions for me?

STAFFING AND SCHEDULE

At a minimum, a fully functional SOC should have one fulltime salaried SOC manager, one salaried SCO supervisor, eight fulltime hourly operators, one to two part-time or flex SCOs, and two to three members of your security officer staff (if applicable) trained as backups and possible replacements when the fulltime employees leave the SOC. This level of staffing will meet any UL required code of having at least two SCOs on duty per shift. They must be fully trained SCOs and the managers should hold onto their training records for UL inspection.

Shift	Title/Wage		Monday through Friday	
Day Shift	SOC Manager	(Salaried)	0730–1600	(Varies regularly)
	SOC Supervisor	(Salaried)	0900–1730	(Varies regularly)
	SCO	(Hourly)	0700–1500	8 hours
	SCO	(Hourly)	0800–1600	8 hours
Evening Shift	SCO	(Hourly)	1500–2300	8 hours
	SCO	(Hourly)	1600–2400	8 hours
Midnight Shift	SCO	(Hourly)	2300–0700	8 hours
	SCO	(Hourly)	2400–0800	8 hours
Weekends			Saturday and Sunday	
(Midnight and Day)	SCO	(Hourly)	2300–1100	12 hours
	SCO	(Hourly)	2400–0800	8 hours
Day	SCO	(Hourly)	0800–1600	8 hours
(Day and Evening)	SCO	(Hourly)	1100–2300	12 hours
	SCO	(Hourly)	1600–2400	8 hours

Why two members of management you ask? Always think about succession in case the SOC manager leaves or "gets hit by a bus" as we used to say often. The supervisor should be a strong enough leader to immediately step in and fill the role at least on an interim basis until the position can be permanently filled. If your SOC becomes fully integrated within in your company, you cannot allow your service to decline if the SOC manager leaves abruptly. The SOC manager should train his or her supervisor to be as knowledgeable and capable of doing the job as they are. Any manager who keeps everything to themselves in the hopes of making themselves feel more valuable, important, or because they think they cannot get fired if they hold all the data is a weak leader. A manager and a supervisor can also take turns being the after-hours on call referred to as "SOC On Call" in this book. This allows both time to decompress if both leaders take turns being the SOC On Call every other week.

If additional training is needed or if there is a problem on an after-hours shift, the supervisor or manager can adjust their schedule accordingly to work with that shift and still have a leader available during the day to respond to upper management or customer's inquiries and requests. Two supervisors also give you the flexibility of being able cover open shifts if several employees give their notices all at one time. You must be ready for that because a SCO position is not something people with ambition tend to stay in for more than a couple of years if you're lucky. Hopefully you're fortunate enough to have a couple of work horses that are quite eager to pick up any open shifts for the overtime pay.

All shifts should be staggered so you don't have everyone coming and going at the same time. When one operator is being relieved, you will still have one operator logged into the systems. Your two permanent day shift SCOs should be two of your best operators on the staff and work Monday–Friday. Most businesses, especially the Fortune 500 companies, will conduct the most activity during the daytime hours and they will need to be skilled, fast, and experienced on a large variety in the ongoing tasks in the SOC such as completing badge access requests and performing simple programming tasks such as new card readers. Your three midnight and evening shift people will take turns rotating on a regular basis through a fixed 3-week rotation. Do not rotate staff from midnight to evening and back. Studies have shown that bouncing around from shift to shift is unhealthy and from our own experience we have found that to be true. Some overtime will be required to vacation and sick days, but there is no way to avoid that in any schedule.

All SCO's should be instructed to arrive at a minimum of 5–10 minutes prior to the start of their shift to allow time, put personal belongings in their provided locker, food in refrigerator, or utilize the restroom prior to their start at the workstation and receiving pass-on information from the SCO being relieved. You should have procedures on what to do if a SCO is not relieved from duty on time. The entire staff should be made to understand that in the event of emergency they may be required to stay past the end of their shift to assist with the emergency or write the incident report. There should also be a policy that states a SCO is not allowed to remain in the SOC after the end of their shift for the sole purpose of socializing because that is a distraction for the SCO's duties that are now on shift.

Schedules should be posted for operators to review and initial at least two weeks prior to the start of the work week. If you are putting out a schedule less than a week prior to the actual start date, you are a not doing your job as a manager or supervisor and making your operators lives more difficult than they need to be. Paid time off (PTO) or vacation requests should be required to submit at a minimum of 30 days in advance. This should give the SOC management team ample time to talk to other SCOs about covering for the operators on PTO. SOC management should not be so rigid to not allow SCOs the opportunity to swap shifts if the shift swap does not create additional overtime and is preapproved by the manager or supervisor. If both parties understand that they must report for their new shift and if one fails that they will both receive verbal or written counseling.

SAMPLE THREE-WEEK ROTATION

In the following pages is an example of a three-week rotation that we created and used in the past. This is a schedule that allows the midnight and evening shift operator a 5-day break with one weekend off every 3 weeks, which helps make up for the fact of working weekends on a regular basis.

Example SOC Schedule I Midnight Shift							
06/01–06/07	MON-1	TUES-2	WED-3	THUR-4	FRI-5	SAT-6	SUN-7
2300–0700 1	SCO 3	SCO 3	SCO 3	SCO 2	SCO 2	2300–1100 SCO 2	2300–1100 SCO 2
	Start Sunday	Start Monday	Start Tues	Start Wed	Start Thurs	Start Friday	Start Saturday
0001–0800 2	SCO 1	SCO 1	SCO 1	SCO 1	SCO 1	SCO 3	SCO 3
Day Shift							
06/01–06/07	MON	TUES	WED	THURS	FRIDAY	SAT	SUN
0700–1500 1	SCO	SCO	SCO	SCO	SCO	NOTES:	
0800–1600 2	SCO	SCO	SCO	SCO	SCO	PART TIME OR SPLIT SHIFT	PART TIME OR SPLIT SHIFT
Evening Shift							
06/01–06/07	MON	TUES	WED	THURS	FRIDAY	SAT	SUN
1500–2300 1	SCO 1	SCO 1	SCO 1	SCO 1	SCO 1	1100–2300 SCO 2	1100–2300 SCO 2
1600–2400 2	SCO3	SCO3	SCO3	SCO 2	SCO 2	SCO3	SCO3

Example SOC Schedule II Midnight Shift

06/08–06/14	MON-8	TUES-9	WED-10	THUR-11	FRI-12	SAT-13	SUN-14
2300–0700 1	SCO 2	SCO 2	SCO 2	SCO 1	SCO 1	2300–1100 SCO 1	2300–1100 SCO 1
	Start Sunday	Start Monday	Start Tues	Start Wed	Start Thurs	Start Friday	Start Saturday
0001–0800 2	SCO 3	SCO 3	SCO 3	SCO 3	SCO 3	SCO 2	SCO 2

Day Shift

06/08–06/14	MON	TUES	WED	THURS	FRIDAY	SAT	SUN
0700–1500 1	SCO	SCO	SCO	SCO	SCO	NOTES:	
0800–1600 2	SCO	SCO	SCO	SCO	SCO	PART TIME OR SPLIT SHIFT	PART TIME OR SPLIT SHIFT

Evening Shift

06/08–06/14	MON	TUES	WED	THURS	FRIDAY	SAT	SUN
1500–2300 1	SCO 3	SCO 3	SCO 3	SCO 3	SCO 3	1100–2300 SCO 1	1100–2300 SCO 1
1600–2400 2	SCO 2	SCO 2	SCO 2	SCO 1	SCO 1	SCO 2	SCO 2

Example SOC Schedule III Midnight Shift

06/15–06/21	MON-15	TUES-16	WED-17	THUR-18	FRI-19	SAT-20	SUN-21
2300–0700 1	SCO 1	SCO 1	SCO 1	SCO 3	SCO 3	2300–1100 SCO 3	2300–1100 SCO 3
	Start Sunday	Start Monday	Start Tues	Start Wed	Start Thurs	Start Friday	Start Saturday
0001–0800 2	SCO 2	SCO 2	SCO 2	SCO 2	SCO 2	SCO 1	SCO 1

Day Shift

06/15–06/21	MON	TUES	WED	THURS	FRIDAY	SAT	SUN
0700–1500 1	SCO	SCO	SCO	SCO	SCO	NOTES:	
0800–1600 2	SCO	SCO	SCO	SCO	SCO	PART TIME OR SPLIT SHIFT	PART TIME OR SPLIT SHIFT

Evening Shift

06/15–06/21	MON	TUES	WED	THURS	FRIDAY	SAT	SUN
1500–2300 1	SCO 2	SCO 2	SCO 2	SCO 2	SCO 2	1100–2300 SCO 3	1100–2300 SCO 3
1600–2400 2	SCO 1	SCO 1	SCO 1	SCO 3	SCO 3	SCO 1	SCO 1

SUPERVISORY AUTHORITY

All SCOs should understand that the SOC manager and the SCO supervisor have the authority to make changes to their schedules and the post orders as necessary to meet the company's goals and provide the appropriate shift coverage to maintain UL certification. SCOs should also be given in writing who else within the company or in the chain-of-command have the right to give the operators orders outside the scope of their post orders such as site security, safety, or facility managers at the locations they are monitoring. The SOC staff should know that at any time in the day or night they are allowed to contact the SOC manager or SCO supervisor for guidance or further clarification duties and objectives.

Any company that has their SOC monitoring multiple locations that also have security officers at several locations and utilize a centralized security department, we recommend that the SOC be your depository of all the security officers location post orders and hold the rank of Sergeant. This authority allows the SOC to dispatch services without question especially during an emergency event and provides the SCOs with the ability to require incident reports be written by the security officer when something happens at their site where they are stationed.

STAFF RESPONSIBILITY

You must make it a requirement through policy and training that all staff members hold the personal responsibility to know and understand the duties, policies, and procedures in place for your SOC. Through the course of time, staff may discover through their regular shift work that requirements have changed and procedures or post orders need to be updated to reflect the latest information or deleted altogether due to the fact the action is no longer required. All staff members should feel free to approach the management with ideas for improvement and point out to SOC management when a procedure has become outdated and needs to be eliminated from the site procedures or SOC post orders. The SOC leadership needs to work hard to ensure that the procedures stay as up-to-date as possible to ensure that all operators have the latest information at their fingertips and they cannot do that without the help of the rest of the staff.

HISTORICAL LESSONS

Your training and procedures must be thorough and easy to find for future reference. Jarpey hired one charming operator who basically pretended to "read" the post orders and charmed his way through the training period. A couple of weeks into working shifts, his coworkers began to say, "this guy doesn't know what he is doing." Jarpey should have listened, because a few days later an emergency event took place at a site and a mass notification was needed per the procedure. Prince charming didn't know what to do and the SOC ended up looking bad. Jarpey states:

> When I sat down with the SCO to talk about what had happened, I first made sure he understood the importance of situation which he stated he did.
> I then asked him why he did not follow the procedure for sending out the mass notification.s His answer "I couldn't find it." This blew my mind because everything was electronic and only three clicks away. That was one of those moments where you sigh, rub your eyes and shake your head. He didn't last too much longer after that.

Treat your people right because you need them. There was a time we had five SCOs who left for various reasons within a 6-week period. We had one operator who worked 90 hours one week and 86 hours the next in a 2-week pay period. Think about that for a second. That is 96 hours of overtime pay. That operator did not have a day off for over a month. There was one day toward the end of the month-long overtime when he came into work and looked like death warmed over. Fearing for his well-being, Jarpey asked him "are you alright?" His reply, "Hey can I get more hours? I want to buy a new truck." You need to appreciate those people who work those extra hours for you. Get them a gift card, buy them lunch, or give them a company appreciation award to show that you recognize their commitment to the team.

CHAPTER 7

Post Orders and Procedures

INTRODUCTION

The purpose of your SOCs post orders and site procedures is to establish an orderly and productive procedural response to all nonemergency, security, fire, and life safety events affecting and reported to your company. Additionally, the post orders must outline the duties required by your SCOs on a regular basis. The post orders you create or have in place must be followed as written unless ordered to do so by authorized personnel. In this chapter, we will provide some of the basics that must be written into your post orders for you to ensure that you are providing your staff with the most detailed procedures and up-to-date information. Not everything can be written down and SCOs will need to adapt to many different situations that are regularly presented to them. But if a task becomes a regular habit then it should be documented on how to complete the task and who it should be reported to for follow up.

SETTING UP YOUR POST ORDERS

Any UL certified central station is required to have paper copies of your post orders and site procedures on hand for SCOs to be able utilize during their shift. Assuming your SOC is UL certified you will need to create your post orders in a word document form that can be printed out, and placed in a binder to meet the UL requirement but to our knowledge no one relies solely on paper anymore. Paper copies of procedures are only if your computers crash. Post orders can easily be broken into eight chapters (see more detailed example provided later in this chapter). Below is the intended purpose for each chapter:

1. *Introduction*—The same information as covered in the previous chapter.
2. *Duties*—All the daily tasks that need to be done and how to do them. New hires will need to refer to this often until the task becomes a habit. Every daily task that is required should be documented and

55

Security Operations Center Guidebook. DOI: http://dx.doi.org/10.1016/B978-0-12-803657-0.00007-6

placed in this chapter which normally becomes the largest chapter in the post orders.

3. *Call center procedures*—This section covers anything that relates to anyone calling into the SOC for information or support.
4. *Emergency procedures*—Depending upon the nature of the business for your organization this could become your most referred to chapter by your SCO's.
5. *Standards and policies*—This section should cover everything from workplace cleanliness to personal hygiene and much more because those things need to dealt with up front for new hires
6. *Equipment procedures*—This section details how to use every software program and piece of equipment in your SOC.
7. *Post order changes and updates*—You may need to change a current post order or add a new one but do not have time to update the printed copy. Place the changes or additions in the book here until the entire post orders can be updated.
8. *Appendices*—Your appendices should include examples of the various checklists used regularly and documents that are required to complete.

There are different ways you could host your electronic post orders and site procedures for all your SCO's to easily access. The goal is to make it as easy as possible for SCOs to find and click on the information they need to review. If they have to click more than four times to find the information they are looking for then it is too difficult and you need to create something more streamlined.

A shared network drive folder that can only be accessed by your team and various individuals within your security organization such as the SOC manager's upper management or support personnel within the security department. If you use this method, your folders need to be organized in a way that makes sense to all the staff and does not require several different clicks to find the information they need. Your procedural documents need to be locked so that SCOs are not making their own editing changes. Only the SOC manager and SCO supervisor should be making changes to post orders and site procedures.

Microsoft SharePoint is another tool that can be used to set up your post orders and site procedures that can be accessed. Unless the SOC manager or the SCO supervisor have the skills to do so this usually requires someone from your IT department with strong SharePoint skills to set up your page to include everything you need. If your IT department can commit to creating this page for you then this is a great way to set your SOC because you can have more on the SharePoint page than just procedural items, you can also include daily activity reports (DARs), incident reports (IRs), and your pass on log. A SharePoint page is also searchable and would make it easier for the SOC management to search reports if they need to conduct a follow up on an event.

Microsoft Outlook contacts can be modified to use as a way to store your post orders and procedures. Outlook would work well with a group email inbox. With Outlook you create a folder for the post orders in numerical order to reflect the chapter and section order of the word document. Create a separate folder for the site procedures and put them in the order that your company uses such as a site number or by city and/or state.

The previous examples are what a large number of companies have available to them but there are also software programs you can purchase that perform these functions for you easily. We know that can it be difficult to convince upper management to spend the money required for purchasing one of these programs but the software can also provide a way to manage your IRs, create metrics and provide trend analytics.

CREATE A SHARED EMAIL ADDRESS FOR SECURITY INQUIRIES AND REQUESTS

Every SOC should have a shared email address for the entire SOC staff to access to be able to respond to your internal and external customers. Too often your customers will email upper security management, the SOC manager, the SCO supervisor, or one of the fulltime SCOs directly and if that person is out of office, on PTO, dealing with an alarm or away from their station the email request will not be handled in a timely manner and customer service satisfaction will drop. Everyone in your company should be taught to email the shared email address directly. Every person in the security department should always turn on their out-of-office reply and ask people to contact the SOC at the shared email if the request is urgent. The SOC then becomes the heartbeat of your company's security department.

PERFORMANCE OF DUTIES

Security personnel often work closely with the ethics, legal, human resources, and communications departments of any company. When working with those groups, the expectation for the SOC and its staff should always be to conduct themselves with the utmost of integrity and character as they perform their duties and tasks. Teach your staff that the daily habits and attitude that they carry toward their work will determine their character as a professional and reflect upon your security organization as a whole. All it takes is one big mistake or one bad employee to cast a negative light on your SOC and the security organization as a whole. Promote teamwork on a regular and consistent basis, because if each shift partner does not work with the other then the team suffers as a whole and you will have customer complaints made against your SOC.

All SCOs should be made aware of and understand the standards that are required for their duties and this should be written into the standards portion of your post orders. A reminder of the basics could even be posted on the wall within the SOC for each SCO to review everyday. Here is an example of what could be posted:

> The duties in our SOC will include a great deal of customer service, working with different people, several different forms of computer software and equipment. You will work with mechanical, intrusion and most importantly fire alarms. You will monitor access and perform remote patrols of sites, even in different states, with our camera monitoring system. As a SCO here, you are expected to promptly assess and respond to alarms and incidents, and most importantly be truthful and factual. You will protect the company and its employees, contractors and guests at all times.
>
> You are never alone. Your shift partner will help answer your questions. If both shift partners are unsure of how to handle a situation, then you should call the SOC On Call.
>
> There will be times when you will have to make quick decisions due to the urgency of the situation. In such cases, good judgment should prevail and follow up communication with the SCO Supervisor, SOC Manager and/or the upper management of your security organization must be made immediately.
>
> Always perform in the most professional manner possible and be a good shift partner.
>
> Always remember the company and its personnel are our customers and we are here to serve their security needs.
>
> Always complete your assigned tasks and duties to the best of your abilities.
>
> Always keep your chain-of-command informed of problems and situations that affect the SOC and its personnel.
>
> Don't hold unnecessary and/or prolonged telephone conversations while on duty, as they distract from your duties, alertness and minimize performance.
>
> Personal electronic device usage in the SOC is forbidden and will be cause for disciplinary action, which could include removal from the account.
>
> Reading of literature or material not connected with your duties, the company or the security industry, unless authorized by a supervisor, is strictly prohibited while on duty.

Horseplay and/or disorderly conduct must be avoided at all times and will be cause for disciplinary action. Such acts are dangerous to the individuals involved and constitute conduct unbecoming of the job and its position.

Do NOT rely on your memory alone; always have a pad of paper and a pen available to write down pertinent information.

Action on or off duty must not be such that it brings unfavorable publicity to the SOC, the company or unfavorable contact with law enforcement agencies.

Do the best you can every day.

EXAMPLE POST ORDER TABLE OF CONTENTS SETUP AND THEIR PURPOSE

Chapter One—Introduction

1. *Welcome to the security operations center*—This welcomes your new employee.
2. *Company mission statement and core values*—Provide information that will help your employee understand your company to include the nature of your business plus the values your company promotes within your industry and the public.
3. *Introduction to your role as a SCO*—The previous standards during the course of work can be placed in this location.
4. *Why the SCO is important*—Explain why their job is important to your organization and the company as a whole.
5. *SCO job description*—Provide a copy of their job description here.
6. *SOC mission statement*—Provide the mission statement here.
7. *SOC post order summary*—Establish the purpose of the post orders the SCOs are required to follow and their areas of responsibility.
8. *SOC supervisory authority*—Describe what authority the SCOs have, who has the authority to override the post orders due to extenuating circumstances and what to do when that happens.
9. *Staffing and schedule*—Write the current staffing requirements and provide an example of the schedule as stated in Chapter 6.
10. *Hours of service*—Explain the hours of service and why it is important to maintain coverage and how to accomplish that. The SOC must have two SCOs per shift, 24 hours a day, 365 days a year and one SCO must be in the SOC at all times. Add what to do if their relief doesn't show for their shift and what to do in the event of family emergency or sudden illness. Above all they must understand that they cannot leave their post until properly relieved by another fully trained SCO.

Chapter Two—Duties

1. *Duties and the SOC on call*—Describe the responsibility of doing their job to best of their ability and who is the primary on call for after-hours questions.
2. *Shift duties in chronological order*—Each shift will have their own duties to perform on a daily basis. This procedure is to ensure the equal distribution of work being performed and should be distributed between each workstation. The goal is not to keep them busy because alarms and customer requests will do that but describe who is in charge of updating the DAR or responding to emails that are received in the shared email inbox.
3. *Daily activity reports (DAR)*—The DAR is crucial to maintaining a log of all activities during the course of the day. It must be constantly updated throughout each shift as events unfold. It is a legal document and should be treated as such. Always remember that if it isn't in writing, then it didn't happen. SCOs should try to be as detailed and specific as possible. Each entry should be noted with the initials of the SCO that created the entry. The most common question about the DAR is, "what should I write?" The best rule to live by is, "when in doubt, write it out!" All DARs should be completed electronically and saved by date in a shared drive folder for each SCO to be able to write in. To ensure simplicity and reduce the amount of forms being created and saved, there should be one DAR for the entire SOC each day. Unless you have a software program for daily reports or are using SharePoint we recommend you use a spreadsheet to accomplish this task. Midnight shift would create a new one from a previously made template at the start of each day and the shift duties describe who would have control for creating new entries into the DAR. Provide the procedure on where to find the template, how to set up, and save the new DAR.
4. *SOC email inbox and inquiries and requests*—This is your group email address that all SCOs can access. The goal is to have emails that are sent to the SOC responded to in less than 2 hours, completed in less than 8 hours' time and should be completed in an absolute maximum of 24 hours. Each shift should respond to and complete each request as fast as possible. The day shift will often be the troubleshooters. If after-hour shifts are just not sure what to do with the request, then they should submit it to the fixed day shift personnel. If a SCO is having a problem helping the customer, or you need someone to make phone contact with the person directly and they work regular day hours, then you should refer the request to the day shift personnel who will often be the troubleshooters since they

are often the most experienced operators. The day shift personnel should always follow up with the after-hours staff on how they were able to solve the problem so those shifts will know for future reference. When the day shift SCOs are having problems then they will work with the SCO supervisor and/or the SOC manager to get the problem solved and get the customer taken care of!

5. *Pass on information*—The passing on of information from one SCO to another SCO is one of the most critical tasks that is performed everyday by your staff. You need to document that pass on's are required and it will become a strong habit. There are three ways pass on's can be conducted.
   a. *Verbal*—When the relieving SCO has arrived they should be briefed on the events of the previous shift, any major incidents, and any tasks that need to be completed. They should be informed of any new policies or procedures that may have been implemented since their last shift.
   b. *Email*—Is a great way to pass on information because it can be written while still fresh in your mind and sent to the appropriate personnel.
   c. *Pass on log or board*—Most security posts have pass on logs but in a SOC using a computer is necessary and email can often replace logs. Having a pass on board placed on a wall in the SOC with highly important information can also be utilized. This allows the oncoming SCO to look at the board in case he forgets the verbal.
   All three have their benefits and could all be utilized at the same time depending upon priority or purpose of the pass on information. The best way to ensure that communication is passed on correctly from shift to shift is to perform all three. It may seem like extra work but you only protect yourself, your coworkers, and the entire reputation of the SOC.

6. *Weekly, monthly, and quarterly reports*—Reviewing access to restricted or others areas is important to ensure that no one is doing anything improper. Whether they want the reports or not, your restricted area owners should receive access history reports for their specific areas. Running history reports is best tasked to the slowest shift, usually the midnight shift. Set your procedures that every Sunday night/Monday morning midnight shift is running reports for the prior week and on the first of each month the midnight shift runs the history report. Sarbanes-Oxley (SOX), DoE, and DoD often require maintaining and monitoring access history of restricted areas.

7. *Site access control*—See Chapter 9, Enterprise Access Control.

8. *Key control*—We are both proponents of card access control for a site's perimeter and any room of importance shared by more than one

person. But each site will always have some form of key control such as keys issued to security officers, various maintenance or other service providers, and individual offices. Your SOC may not be issuing the keys but they should know the procedures for your security officers in case the officers call the SOC for guidance. You should have procedures in place that answer who is authorized for any key, and how that issuance is recorded.

9. *Maintenance issues and condition reports*—Create a procedure for what to do if a security officer reports a maintenance issue, or if the SOC sees an issue on a camera such as a water leak. All maintenance issues reported through security should be catalogued in a database as a condition report.

10. *Special projects*—Your SOC will always have special projects. The dayshift should not be expected or required to complete everything. Spread the workload to the off-hours shifts such as bulk access card printing jobs, large access control projects, researching information for the corporate security department or the SOC, reviewing camera video to try and find a particular incident. Write in your post orders that regular SOC duties come first and special projects second. It should be required that they report why they could not complete a project on time if they were too busy performing regular SOC duties.

11. *Investigative support*—The SOC should be a primary supporter for any company investigator because they can run history reports, archive and review video, plus provide past incident reports of any significance to the case. All SCOs should know that any investigative support provided to a company investigator is completely confidential and should not be shared with anyone outside of the SOC. If someone were to discuss a case with someone outside of the SOC without prior permission from the investigator or the SOC chain-of-command that they would be subject to termination.

12. *Communication department*—If your company has a communications department create a procedure on how to contact someone from that department in the event that they need to be notified of a situation or media request.

13. *News media*—What should your staff do if the media calls, or arrive at one of your locations? Most likely your procedure will be to call the communications department but if you do not have one then you should have a plan in place of how to handle the media.

14. *Corporate safety*—How will your SOC interact with your company safety department? If your SOC is the primary for reporting incidents such as medical emergencies or accidents that result in injuries on the job, have a procedure in place that dictates who will be notified and how.

15. *Information technology department*—The IT department is one of the most valuable allies in performing the duties in the SOC. All SCOs need to know how to contact the IT staff 24 hours a day in the event that a computer or server goes down that affects the performance of the SOC.

16. *Human resources*—The SOC should know whom to contact and for what reason, if there is an issue with staff for any reason. The human resources (HR) termination procedure should be intertwined with the SOC. HR should know to contact the SOC immediately after the termination of any employee because they are there 24 hours a day.

17. *Legal department*—Create a procedure for how the legal department should be contacted in the event of a process server. Work with someone in the legal department to determine exactly what they would want to be notified right away of what can be just an email notification.

18. *Add as necessary*—Every company is different and will have their own company-specific nuances and procedures that must be recorded. This section of your post orders can grow as large as you want it. You cannot write a procedure for everything but if it is a regular occurrence then you should have something in writing. It is important to stress to your SCOs that they are not required to remember the procedures verbatim. They should know that you expect them to know where to find the information and the proper procedure when they need to utilize it.

Chapter Three—Call Center Procedures

1. *Security systems*—A centralized enterprise access control system will receive many calls related to equipment not working properly such as doors not unlocking when card is presented. The procedure should start with SCO's utilizing a troubleshooting checklist to determine the nature of the issue and then what to do to rectify the issue such as putting in a service ticket to your systems integrator. A SOC troubleshooting checklist will be provided in the appendix. If your security department is centralized, the SOC might be the first call from a site manager who wants to install new security equipment. Have a procedure in place for what information they should capture and who it should be passed on to for getting the new systems in place.

2. *Incident reports (IR)*—Employees may call the SOC to report an incident that took place at their site if different from your SOC location. The SOC staff should be trained and have procedures on what to do when receiving an IR how to document and catalog the IR into the incident

reporting database and who should be notified regarding the incident. These calls could include but are not limited to:

a. Emergency services are called or just show up
b. Theft
c. Threat
d. Damage to property such as accident or vandalism
e. Hazardous material or waste spill
f. Ethics violation
g. Firearms use
h. Any criminal activity
i. Major incidents
j. Customer complaint about your company
k. External complaints against your company such as a company truck driver weaving in the road.

Writing the incident in a factual manner leaving out opinions and personal beliefs must be mandatory because these documents could end up in a court of law. Your staff has to act like junior investigators while on the phone with internal or external customers asking questions from the reporting party to ensure that they have all the facts of the incident being reported. Teach your staff to always ask one last question when taking incident reports, "is there anything else you can think of that may be important to know regarding this matter? Anything at all?"

3. *Mass notification alert system*—If your company has a mass notification system, your SOC should be at the heart of that system. You should have procedures in place that describes what kind of alerts that can be sent out and who is authorized to send those alerts. Distribution lists (DL) could include site, regional, or business unit breakdowns. Every SCO should know how find who is authorized to have the SOC send out and alert and to who or which different DLs.

4. *Add as necessary*—Depending upon the nature of your company's business, there are several other items that could be included in this section such as:

a. Site specific call out of personnel
b. Vehicle accident reports
c. Claims against your company
d. Fitness for duty calls such as supervisor calling to inform that he or she believes that their employee in unfit for duty
e. IT-related warnings and alerts

Chapter Four—Emergency Procedures

1. *Emergency preparedness*—In an emergency, in any company events occur that stress the capabilities of the people, equipment, and

systems that are in place. While planning can be conducted for expected disasters such as severe weather, sometimes all the planning and procedures cannot get you ready for when something is actually happening. Place in your post orders that you understand this and that they should try to remain calm, professional, and document everything that happens.

2. *Emergency notifications*—Your post orders should contain who is to be notified in the event of an emergency whether by site, region, or business unit.

3. *Emergency plan*—You need to have an emergency plan in case your SOC is required to evacuate the building they are located, which could be due to many things such as a gas leak or fire. If you have a backup location to move to or activate, this should be written in detail here.

4. *Fire*—Your SOC needs a plan on what to do if there is a fire. UL requires that tarps be placed over alarm monitoring equipment. If your SOC is UL certified to monitor fire alarms, this section is a good place to put basic alarm monitoring and response procedures to fire alarms.

5. *Medical emergencies*—Procedures should be in place for receiving medical emergency alerts inside the SOC's building, and at other sites with and without security officers.

6. *Severe weather*—What to do in the event of severe weather such as tornado.

7. *Power outage*—What to do in the event of a building power outage at any site location.

8. *Phone outage*—What to do if the SOC's location loses phone capabilities. UL certification requires you have a backup phone and most central stations keep a cell phone on site for those moments.

9. *Suspicious parcel*—What should the SOC do if the mailroom calls and states they have received a suspicious package.

10. *Workplace violence*—Describe what to do if the SOC receives a report of potential or actual workplace violence.

11. *Elevator emergency*—Building elevators often have phones or intercoms these days and these can be programmed to call into your SOC. Procedures need to be in place instructing staff how to handle and what to do.

12. *Trespassers on company property*—Have a procedure that details how to handle a trespasser at any company location and that authorizes your SOC staff to call the police without hesitation.

13. *Civil disturbance: Strikes, protests, or demonstrations*—Is your company prone to strikes, protests, or other civil disturbances? If yes, write a procedure for how those should be handled and who should be notified.

14. *DHS National Terrorism Advisory System*—In the United States or other countries, is your company considered part of critical infrastructure? Then you might be required to take further action in the event that the Department of Homeland Security (DHS) or other government bodies raise the alert level due to potential terrorism. Your SOC should be monitoring news 24/7 so they should know right away that an alert has been issued and needs to take action.

Chapter Five—Standards and Policies

1. *SOC and cleanliness*—This can be one of your most important chapters of your post orders. Laying the policy of workstation cleanliness and shared area usage such as a refrigerator or kitchen area.

2. *Personal hygiene: The difficult topic*—Many central stations are tiny little rooms with two or more people working in close relation to each other. You must write that your SOC staff should understand that everyone has bodily smells and that it is important to prevent subjecting your shift partner to them by not bathing or showering prior to work. It is also important to promote not wearing large amounts of overpowering perfume or cologne that could be agitating to someone else. Write that it is okay for an employee relieving another to immediately wipe down the workstation to prevent the sharing of germs that could infect another employee. They should not be offended when that happens. Wiping down a workstation before you take it over should be the norm because this will help prevent the spread of infectious germs and reduce the calling off sick factor.

3. *Uniform dress code*—Write exactly what the dress code is for your SOC. Try to be as detailed as possible. Any room for interpretation will result in personnel wearing items that they should not be wearing.

4. *HOW you communicate*—This may seem like a strange chapter to place in your post orders but is critical to the success of your SOC. Your staff must understand that communication is a professional skill that must be constantly honed and crafted. Describe the proper greeting when answering the phone in your SOC and make sure they answer the phone that way each time. Write about practical phone etiquette and the do's and don'ts such as staying away from talking about things such as politics or religion with customers calling into the SOC. Remind your staff that they should appreciate their customers whether internal or external and not become cynical when answering the same questions repeatedly. Teach your staff by writing in your post orders that it is encouraged and required to ask questions when working with customers. Teach your staff to use professional phrases versus informal phrases.

5. *Public relations*—Teach your staff that when dealing with the public they are representatives of the company and that it is important to make a good impression. They should be courteous, sound competent, use tact and discretion. Teach your staff to never say they do not know something. They should always tell customers they will get back to them as soon as possible with an answer.

6. *SOC security and personal safety*—This section should describe what is the proper procedure for someone to enter the SOC with authorization that does not work there and how visitors must be properly identified before entry and signed in upon entry. Staff should be instructed to never give out any personal information or scheduling info about anyone working in the SOC.

7. *Personal electronic devices*—This rule must be strictly enforced and all SCOs must understand that their personal electronic devices are NOT allowed in the SOC. You should write out the list to include the following:
   a. Cell phones or tablets
   b. Laptops or other computer devices
   c. Jump or flash drives
   d. Digital or film cameras or camcorders
   e. Personal televisions
   f. DVD or VHS players
   g. CD or tape players
   h. Radios
   i. MP3 players (Apple, Sony, SanDisk, etc.)
   j. Handheld gaming devices (Gameboy, PlayStation Portable, iPod touch, etc.)
   k. Gaming consoles (Xbox, PlayStation, Nintendo, etc.)

8. *Email and Internet policy*—All SOC staff should know that they have no privacy when it comes to their work email and web surfing. They should not be allowed to access personal email while at work to include Gmail, Yahoo, Outlook, or other Internet email providers. This chapter could also describe various email standards or show what the required auto signature is for SCOs on their work email.

9. *Proprietary information*—This policy is needed to explain that they are required to protect company proprietary information at all times.

10. *Break policy*—Describe the break policy. How long are they allowed to be gone? Where exactly are they allowed to go while on break? How quickly must they be able to return in case of emergency? These questions must be answered in this section and thorough as possible to remove room for additional interpretation.

11. *Tobacco policy*—Describe the tobacco policy. Is tobacco even allowed on the property? If so, where are they allowed to smoke? What about smokeless tobacco? These questions must be answered in this section.

12. *Leaving the SOC? Carry the cell phone or radio!*—Anytime a SCO leaves the SOC for a restroom break or other reason, they should be required to carry the SOC cell phone or site radio in the event something major happens and their shift partner needs to call them back to the SOC as soon as possible (ASAP) for assistance.

13. *Television policy*—Every SOC we've run has had cable news running 24/7 in the SOC. If there is an event that could affect your company, the news could be the first way you find out. But if you have cable news you'll have other channels available and you must describe what is allowable to watch such as local or national news networks and weather channels. You may need to write what volume level is acceptable because some SCOs might want to turn the volume up to where it is too loud and distracting. It is recommended that you lock all channels that are not allowed for viewing during a shift to remove any temptation to watch the National Football League (NFL), movies, or other nonwork-related channels.

Chapter Six—Equipment Procedures

1. *Physical Access Control System (PACS)*—Every PACS has a help button and a user guide but they are usually loaded with extra verbiage that is not helpful or they do not provide enough visuals to explain how to get from point A to point B. In your procedures create personalized examples of how to do everything from acknowledging an alarm, programming an access card, or programming a reader into the system by using pictures to explain everything that is needed to do step by step. Be sure to include procedures for how to:
   a. Acknowledge an alarm.
   b. View the details of an alarm.
   c. View a map of the alarms location.
   d. Resetting an alarm.
   e. Work with auxiliary outputs.
   f. Manual, timed, or conditional commands to devices.
   g. Running activity, history, locator, muster, and access card listing reports.
   h. How to read and understand a cardholder's profile and status.
   i. How to assign access to a cardholder.
   j. How to add, modify, or delete a card reader or monitor point.

2. *Video surveillance system*—Create procedures that simplify how to log in, set up cameras for monitoring, how to pan, tilt, or zoom a camera, how to review video, how to archive video for review at a later date or time.

3. *Workstation phones*—All phone systems are different and your SCOs need to know how to log into your phone system, place calls on hold, transfer calls and conference calls together. If you have a call coding

system, you will need a procedure on how to code your calls after a call is completed.

4. *Audio recording system*—If your SOC is monitoring fire or burglar alarms, you should have an audio phone recording system to record all your calls coming in and going out. This is necessary for your operators to review calls for their incident reports to ensure that they are documenting detailed information.

5. *Any piece of equipment or software the SOC uses*—This section could grow to be the largest of your post orders depending on the number of different pieces of equipment and software packages you use on a regular basis in your SOC. These are basically your cheat sheets for your operators to follow until the steps are committed to memory. Other procedures to consider adding if you have them:
   a. PACS servers operating and troubleshooting
   b. SOC cell phone or handheld radio
   c. Intercom system for your building
   d. Fax machine if still used
   e. Your local fire panel if your SOC is responsible for it.

Chapter Seven—Post Order Changes and Updates

Your hard copy of the post orders should be kept in a three-ring binder for easy removal of expired and additions of new or updated post orders. Printing a whole new set of post orders is unnecessary until you have several changes already completed. Temporarily post changes and new additions here until the entire post order book or binder can be updated.

Chapter Eight—Appendices

In your appendix section, provide good examples of regularly used checklists and other documents.

   A. Troubleshooting checklist for the PACS.
   B. Bomb-threat checklist
   C. Example Schedule.
   D. Example Time sheet.
   E. Example of a well-written and properly completed incident report.
   F. Example of a well-written and properly completed daily activity report.
   G. Chain-of-command diagram for the SOC and above.

SITE PROCEDURES

For every site you have within your system you need to create a specialized site-specific procedure saved in a location where each operator can easily find it both electronically and hard copy if necessary. For any new site that you add into your system, your SOC should be provided the following information:

- Site security manager or other responsible party provides information to SOC about new site.
- This should include restricted (RST) area info.
- Alarm expectations.
- Contacts with numbers.
- Knox box info or other exterior information for fire department response.
- Special instructions regarding the site.

The SOC manager should never be the responsible party for approving the final draft of the site procedure. The local site security manager or facility manager should be the final person to approve a site procedure. Having a local authority approve the procedure validates that the information written is correct and is the proper way to handle a situation. This document should include the following information:

Section One—Site Info

- a. Name of site.
- b. Region or business unit affiliated with.
- c. Address of sites.
- d. All phone numbers affiliated with the site.
- e. List of restricted areas within the location and their owners.
- f. A notes section that could include any random note of pertinent information that would be important for operators to know.
- g. Normal working business hours and their schedule.
- h. Maps of location and floors.

Section Two—Intrusion Alarm Response

How to handle an intrusion alarm step by step and the actions that are necessary to take to complete an alarm response.

Section Three—Fire Alarm Response

How to handle a fire alarm step by step and the actions that are necessary to take to complete a fire response.

Section Four—Mechanical Alarms

How to handle a mechanical alarm step by step and the actions that are necessary to take to complete a mechanical alarm response.

Section Five—Contact Lists

This should include your regular business hour contacts, your after-hours contacts, key site management personnel, and all the emergency services number that are applicable to that site.

Section Six—Special Instructions

Each site will have their own unique synchronicities and may require one or more special instructions that require a different action than those already documented in the site procedure.

This document can always grow as necessary if there are more specialized instructions to ensure that each site works well with the SOC. Part of that is through the partnership of working with the local site management to ensure that the proper procedures are being followed. Each site manager should understand that the site procedure will only change if the site informs the SOC of changes at the location.

For current locations in your system your site procedures should be updated annually at a minimum or on an as-needed basis. This is a task that can easily be assigned to one of your dayshift operators who can easily attempt to contact the site security manager during regular working hours to verify that the procedures are still correct.

HISTORICAL LESSONS

Post orders is one of the most difficult tasks for SOC management because they will always need modification and updating to ensure that your staff is following the proper procedures, especially if you have several new hires working. But make sure your staff does not have the capability to make their own modifications to the post orders as they see fit. At one SOC, we had a major change completed by IT and that modified everyone's permissions giving all SOC staff the ability to modify the post orders as they see fit without us knowing about it. But the SOC staff knew it and decided not to share that information. One time a midnight SCO missed a regular daily task and when they realized their mistake, they simply changed the daily task schedule in their post order to remove the task from their schedule, which was conducting a system status check of the site video servers and cameras. It's considered important. When a camera was found offline later that morning the Lead SCO checked the DAR and because the system status check was not noted in the DAR had to begin to review when video was lost, which was before the system status check should have taken place. When the midnight SCO was questioned about it, he simply stated "it's not in the post orders."

The Lead SCO knowing full well that the task is in the post orders was about to lose their mind when the midnight SCO said "check the post orders." So, the Lead did check and discovered that the task was gone. After a further investigation revealed that the last IT data archive backup showed that the task was there in the document previously and the last person to modify the post order was the midnight SCO we knew we had a problem with. When the midnight SCO was presented with the evidence, he was asked "why did you modify the post order instead of just admitting your mistake?" He pleaded the fifth amendment. Seriously. He left to pursue other opportunities.

Training Programs

INTRODUCTION

Your central station post orders and procedures provide the information and standards to your operators who need to know or have on hand to quickly refer to when to perform their duties. Training your operators is when they learn to utilize the post orders and procedures information that is available to them and necessary to perform their duties. You will need to determine how long to train them for, create a schedule for their training to ensure they see all the shifts, what they need to accomplish the training objectives and create an individual training checklist. Training should be never ending for your central station. As the manager of your SOC, you should always continue to create or present new and challenging training classes or tasks to conduct while they work for your staff. That additional level of training allows them to grow as professionals and understand their job that much more. In this chapter, we will cover the different ways to accomplish this goal.

GETTING STARTED

If you have hired your new full-time operator and they start in 2 weeks, what do you need to have ready for them? Human resources and perhaps other areas such as safety may be involved in new hire orientation and you should plan accordingly with each department but we will only focus on the new hire trainee needs for working in the SOC. You will have to prepare ahead of time by getting the new hire their computer accounts requested and set up so that they are ready to log in on day 1 if possible. Get the supplies ready they will need such as a three-ring binder for storing training material and notes, plus a notebook and pen. Their employee mailbox and locker if applicable should be ready for and assigned to them on first day. You are making a statement of your company's professionalism to your new employee by showing how ready you are when they arrive.

Security Operations Center Guidebook. DOI: http://dx.doi.org/10.1016/B978-0-12-803657-0.00008-8

NEW HIRE TRAINING SCHEDULE

Day 1 should always be about basic orientation with the SOC manager during the day even if the employee has been hired to work midnights or evenings. It allows SOC management to get to know the new hire better and talk in more detail about the expectations you have of them. An important idea to impress upon the new hire is that they do not need to remember all of the information they are about to introduced to, they just need to remember where to be able to find it. You show them where the break area is, vending machines, the refrigerator, the restrooms, introduce them to key facility or management personnel. The amount of time that is dedicated to training depends on the amount of work there is to learn during the training. Most Fortune 500 companies that have their own SOCs or central stations should dedicate at least 2 weeks minimum to training the new hire prior to the trainee before they work. For the purpose of this book, we will use 2 weeks as the standard but we would always recommend more training time if possible. Your day shift crew is usually the best employees your SOC has to offer so you will have the new hire to start training with your day shift personnel for at least 3 days. Then for the next 5 days you will have to arrange their schedule so that they spend 1 or 2 days on the opposite shift of which they were hired and 3 or 4 days on the shift they were hired to work. The last 2 days should be back on the day shift so that the SOC manager or supervisor can review the completion of the checklist and ensure the new hire feels comfortable with what they have recently learned before they are added to the regular shift schedule.

INDIVIDUAL TRAINING CHECKLIST

Your training checklist is the heart of your training program. What is the main purpose of the individual training checklist (ITC)? To capture in writing every little step of each task that an employee in your SOC must be familiar with, know where to find the information and are able to perform the tasks they have learned while on duty. Your ITC should mirror many if not all the items found in the post orders but it does not stop there. You must remember to add training items that help to explain how the phones work or how to log on to the computer. That may seem ridiculous to some of you reading this but there are different phone systems and computer operating systems. Not everyone knows the difference among Apple OS, Windows 10, and a Linux platform but if they already know the product then that portion of your training program will be quickly completed.

Managers and SOC operators cannot possibly remember to train a new employee on everything that is needed to learn by memory alone. Even if you are at one of the few companies that has a full-time trainer on staff, they cannot commit all of the tasks that a new hire needs to memory. You must create a list that includes each item that needs to be covered. The more detail you have the better the training the new hire receives and reduces their potential to claim, "I was never taught that." Next to each item are boxes that provide spaces for the trainer to initial then date after the training is completed and the trainee to initial that they have completed the training. The trainee should only initial each line when they feel that they fully understand the task that has been shown to them. There are three steps to good training—explanation, demonstration, and practical application. Your trainers should explain and demonstrate each item the new hire is being shown, then allow the new hire to apply that newly trained skill themselves through practical application.

When your new hire is given the ITC, explain carefully to them that each item they see on the ITC. They have the responsibility of initialing each item only after they understand. The reason for making this very clear is to ensure that after they start working their own shifts and when a mistake is made they cannot say "I didn't really understand that."

Here are some of the main items that every ITC should include for any SOC:

1. Manager or Supervisor orientation. Your day 1 orientation should be on the checklist.
2. Reading the Post Orders. As boring as that may be for a new hire on day 1, they should read through the post orders paper version and be shown how to find the post orders electronically on the computer station.
3. Policies and standards. Another item for day 1 is to ensure the new hire understands the policies and standards in the SOC such as dress code and break policy.
4. Access Control System (ACS). Usually the most important next to alarm and camera monitoring. Write down every possible part of the ACS your operator needs to be familiar with. The more detail on the page the better the training the new hire receives.
   a. Log on and off
   b. Alarm identification
   c. Alarm acknowledgment
   d. Alarm notification
   e. Alarm instructions
   f. Alarm comments
   g. Cardholder files
      i. Opening Card Holders
      ii. Discussing each and every tab in a cardholder file
      iii. Adding comments to a cardholder

        iv. Adding New cards

        v. Deactivating cards access

        vi. Modifying access

        vii. Deleting old cards

    h. How to open Doors and Gates with the ACS

    i. How to run reports and send to customers in various formats

        i. Activity Reports—Group and Individual

        ii. History Reports

        iii. Muster Reports

        iv. Running reports to PDF and Excel.

    j. How to Check Status of ACS Equipment

        i. Readers

        ii. Monitoring points

        iii. Panels and how to download the latest information

5. Video Monitoring System (VMS). If your VMS is the same brand and software as your ACS, then your training is easier with only one product to learn. Most companies will have two separate systems and you will have to train your staff to work with both. There are benefits to both ways of operation and these will be discussed in Chapter 11, Enterprise Video Surveillance.

    a. Logging on and off

    b. Site or recorder selection

    c. Setting up Live views from multiple recorders

    d. PTZ operations and preset usage

    e. Review recorded video

    f. Video motion alarms and how to acknowledge them

    g. How to create and save a video clip

    h. Archive recorded video for future reference

    i. How to send video screen shots and full segments to customers.

6. Fire alarm monitoring if applicable. To monitor fire at your location, you will need to be Underwriters Laboratories (UL) code 827 certified and in compliance with the National Fire Protection Association (NFPA) code 72. There is a significant cost in setting up fire alarm monitoring because they require different alarm receiving equipment than your ACS, back up alarm receiving equipment, an uninterruptible power supply system that lasts for 4 hours' minimum and this also requires two people to be on duty 24/7 per shift. There is an annual cost to be inspected by UL on an annual basis to ensure you are in compliance with the code but that should be considered a good thing because you only learn from where you have findings. Smaller companies will have their SOCs focus solely on security and have third party central stations monitor the fire alarms. Fire monitoring from a proprietary perspective can save a company

money in the form of reduced monitoring fees. This would benefit larger companies with multiple locations needing fire monitoring services. If your company owns and operates 50–100 sites, you are spending close to $1000 dollars per site annually or more. That $50–100k a year can be reduced by bringing that fire monitoring in house. Whatever upfront costs there are will be paid back after a few years. When dealing with fire life safety, we cannot stress enough how important it is to live by the UL 827 code and NFPA 72 and that your training revolves around your staff being able to quickly react to and process fire alarms. Failure to do so could result in loss of life or property.

7. Mass notification system. Many companies have mass notification or crisis alert systems to help alert their employees to situations that are taking place on the property or within the company. There are a wide range of reasons for its use such as power outage, severe weather, or even worse an active shooter in the building. The situation when an alert has to be sent out can be tense depending upon what is the need for the alert. If the alert is due to a fire or an active shooter, your operator is going to be nervous. Create message templates of all the possible alerts you might use because that will make it easier for your SCO to send out an alert quickly.
   a. Location of User Guide or Reference Manual
   b. How to log into the system
   c. How to adjust preferences
   d. How to create a new alert or with a template
   e. How to modify an alert template before sending out.

8. Local fire panel. If the location of your SOC has a local fire panel for monitoring and it is physically located in the SOC then you need to create training steps for how to read, acknowledge alarms, reset alarms, and work with that fire panel.

9. Telephone operations. Too often managers make the mistake of assuming a phone is just a phone and that everyone knows how to use it. As stated earlier, that is not the case because there are many different brands of telephones out there with very different features and functionality. Your training should be written to introduce the new operator to your phone system plus discuss what is the proper communication and phone etiquette while on duty. Your employees need to know what is the proper and/or expected way to answer the phone. They need to know how to answer the call, place the call on hold, transfer the call to another person, or how to create a conference call. You should also have a system to be able to code a call after an answered call has been completed. What is that for? Call tracking and your SOC statistics will be discussed more in

Chapter 17, Metrics. Coding should not be more than eight or nine categories at the most for simplification so SCOs only use one number to code a call to increase speed.

10. Audio recorder playback. We strongly recommend that your SOC have phone call recording capabilities. Check state laws on the requirements for phone call recording. The main reason is for detail verification and ensuring that what gets written into a report is what was stated on the phone call versus what an operator might remember compared to what they wrote down for notes during the call. The other benefit for call recording is protection. In a larger company, you will have people claim they told you something or that you did not tell them something important. It can be very satisfying for a manager to produce a copy of the recording to upper management that exonerates your SOC and proves the other party is wrong. Write your procedures so that each operator can:
    a. How to log into the system
    b. Playback a current or past call
    c. Send a recorded call via email.

11. Hand held radio operations. If your SOC has radios to communicate with security officers, then your staff needs to know how to use them even if they use a microphone stand in the SOC. The SCOs should be taught about proper radio etiquette and brevity codes that are the norm within your company.

12. Intercom system. If the SOC oversees the intercom system for the building you are in, then the SCOs need to know how to operate it.

13. Overhead public address (PA) system. If the SOC controls the PA system in their building, then they should be taught how to use it. The previous item and this one may seem minor to worry about but the goal is to ensure you are covering as many of the SOC topics as possible.

14. Contact information. There should be a list both electronically and on paper that every SCO can find quickly with all the possible contact numbers they might need to call in the event of an emergency or other major incident.

15. Incident reports (IR). If you are still using paper to write IRs we strongly recommend you begin using a computer immediately. Whether you have a software program for an IR database or are simply using word or excel, your staff must be taught how to create, write, document, log, and save your reports.

16. Condition reports. Same as IRs but condition reports focus on safety hazards, mechanical failures, and building maintenance-related issues.

17. Daily activity reports (DAR). Again, if you are still using paper to write DARs, we strongly recommend you begin using a computer

immediately. The DAR is one of the most important documents in an SOC because it should contain all the major activities that took place during the course of an operators shift. This document allows the previous shift to review or search for an incident when they are need of more information.

18. Company computer system. New hires need to know about your company's computer system, the requirements, the do's and don'ts and where to find things such as your word processor or other software.

19. Work Orders or Service Tickets. In our experience that fastest way to ensure that a ticket is created and completed by a vendor is to have your SOC create the ticket in a database and follow up until the problem has been rectified.

20. Inquiries and Requests. Your staff needs to know how to handle any incoming inquiries or requests for service via email.

21. Printers. Although we prescribe to electronic documentation, we know that at times a paper document will be needed and every printer is different. Your staff must know how to utilize the printer they have available to them.

22. Restricted area procedures. No company allows every employee to go into every area that is within a building. Your ACS helps to ensure that only authorized personnel are allowed to access the proper areas. Any room or area that requires limited access should be considered a restricted area and labeled as such in your ACS as RST. Your operators then need to be taught on the proper way to provide access. We'll cover more of this in the next chapter.

23. Site access control. Create a documented process for site access control so that there is a standard to follow. Again, we'll touch more on this in the next chapter.

24. Call center procedures. Go through each post order policy one at a time to ensure the new hire understands the expectations completely.

25. Emergency procedures. You must train the new SCO the same as Call Center procedures.

26. Day shift duties review. Each shift will have a regular set of duties they must perform which should be written out in your post orders. If your new hire is going to start on Midnight shift, then only an introduction is needed for the day shift. Focus their shift duty training on the shift they will be assigned to and spend only a small amount of time introducing them to the duties of the other shifts.

27. Evening shift duties review. Focus their shift duty training on the shift they will be assigned to and spend only a small amount of time introducing them to the duties of the other shifts.

28. Midnight shift duties review. Focus their shift duty training on the shift they will be assigned to and spend only a small amount of time introducing them to the duties of the other shifts.
29. Site procedures review. The trainee should review each site they are responsible for monitoring or providing service and support. Every site is different within a company especially one that has several different types of buildings such as production plants, service centers, or plain office buildings.
30. Latest training information. Always leave blank lines available to write in brand new training that might be introduced while the new hire is training.
31. Add as you feel necessary. What has been written here is only to get you started. Do not limit your ITC to these items alone. Each company is different and new hire personnel will need to be introduced to as much as possible when they start working for your company in your SOC. Think about what you need to add to your training checklist.

The ITC allows you and your staff to ensure the new hire has been properly trained. When the ITC has been completed each primary trainer along with SOC management along with the new hire verifying that they have been trained on the following items. Not every person who gets hired should stay in the SOC. Occasionally you will hire that person who just doesn't get something, cannot handle the responsibilities or pressure involved for whatever reason. You should have a probationary period that allows you to terminate someone's employment from your SOC if they are not meeting the requirements of the job. Having an ITC from the start reduces the possibility of the person blaming you for lack of training them and having them sign the ITC at the completion of their training verifies their understanding of that.

MONTHLY, QUARTERLY, AND ANNUAL TRAINING

Depending upon work flow, time available, and company needs, you should conduct additional training on a regular basis. Certain UL codes require you to conduct training at regular intervals specifically to the code that you are certified under and document all of that training for annual inspection. But it does not have to stop there. If there is internal or external online training tool available to help your employees understand the needs of the company at a greater level, you should take the time to provide that training to the SCOs whether its free or perhaps cost some money. You can easily create your own training by reading books on different skills, leadership or teamwork and write up questions for each chapter. Then require them to read the book during down time while on the job and answer the questions you created.

Never stop training your staff and never stop pushing them to learn more about the job. They will only become better employees for you and your company and they will grow to become better professionals.

HISTORICAL LESSONS

One thing about training is no matter how detailed your training program and ITC are, there is always going to be someone that just doesn't get it. During the probationary period while on the job you will begin to see where they are failing and hopefully on the spot corrections can be made to which they easily respond and can implement the procedural task properly. There will be times that will not happen and you'll be conducting counseling in the office. There will be times you have SCOs stare at you angrily or look at you like you're stupid, perhaps cry due to their perceived failures or yell at you because your system is too difficult to learn.

However, if you listen to the new hire you might occasionally learn that you are forgetting an important detail. One new hire we had was a stellar employee that caught on quickly and we were happy that we found a good one. Plus, this new hire got along great with everyone but didn't like to make small talk of any kind at all. Just did his work very professionally so the rest of the staff respected and gave him his space. One little quirk he had was that he ate his meals cold every day never heated them for over 3 weeks. One time in the breakroom we finally asked "why do eat all your meals cold?" It was obvious the question annoyed him greatly and we got one of "those" looks. Jarpey stated, "why don't you use the microwave in the other room?" His eyes got wide and he replied "there's a microwave we can use?" <sigh> During his training, no one bothered to show him where the microwave was located. That was added to the ITC before the end of the day.

CHAPTER 9

Enterprise Access Control

INTRODUCTION

Companies that use a corporate-wide enterprise PACS need to have policies and controls in place both at the corporate and the SOC level. All employees, contractors, and visitors should be required to wear ID badges while on company property. The employees and contractor's ID badges should be the same as their access badge and work only with the enterprise PACS. No one should ever share an access card at any time for any reason.

The SOC should be the first line in controlling access into all card reader areas, restricted and nonrestricted. The SCO needs to know how access is requested and enforce those guidelines. It is the job of the SOC to control that access by working with the local, regional, or business unit site management. The SOC is there to help the site security or facility managers and restricted area owners regulate the amount of access to their site or restricted area. In this chapter, we will discuss how to set up your PACS; how to handle card access programming and control; how to handle remote site access control; how to set up and control your restricted areas; the importance of system status checks; and troubleshooting problems.

SETTING UP YOUR PHYSICAL ACCESS CONTROL SYSTEM

To make access control easier for a company, have each location entered into the PACS separately. If you are a company in multiple states, name the site segment starting with the state abbreviation followed by the name of the site that the employees use and not what your vendor decides to program into the PACS. If employees call a site, the "General Office" that is how it should be programmed into the PACS versus "Company HQ" as a vendor might decide how to put in there. This will do nothing but confuse your staff when they are receiving calls from people stating they are at the "General Office" and only see company HQ in the system. If the employees at the General

83

Security Operations Center Guidebook. DOI: http://dx.doi.org/10.1016/B978-0-12-803657-0.00009-X

Office call a door with a card reader on it the "West Side Door" then the reader should be labeled the same name and not "Door 3" as an installer might label the door. Ensuring that the SOC and the site are using the nomenclature will improve communications between your SOC and your internal customers at the site.

Working with the site facility or security manager, determine what is the default access that any employee or contractor may be granted on a Monday–Friday basis during regular working hours without prior approval. This usually includes the main entrance and similar doors like a patio door where an employee might go outside on their break. Depending upon your company's line of business you may not be able to set up a basic default for each location that can be given without some form of authorization, and the basic default will still need to receive prior approval from someone with authority over the location.

OPERATOR PERMISSIONS

Your SOC staff should not all have the same permissions across the board until they have proven that they can properly handle the basics changes of card access. Giving a new SOC operator higher permissions in the PACS system to change readers or panels, when they do not have the proper experience to even change access on a card, is asking for problems that do not need to happen. Create levels that each operator must work toward achieving for gaining new system permissions within your PACS. Whether an operator receives higher permissions within the PACS usually depends on the operator and their capabilities as they learn. A simple way to set up the access permissions is creating different layers that can be assigned as your operators prove themselves capable. Such as:

1. *SCO Level I*—Basic card access changes capabilities to include add, modify, or delete access.
2. *SCO Level II*—This level adds the ability to add new, modify, or delete card holders, change reader or panel names, and similar programming.
3. *SCO Level III*—This level adds the ability to create new readers or panels and other items in the PACS.
4. *ADMIN*—This permission level should be reserved for the most trusted of personnel and management.

CARD ACCESS PROGRAMMING AND CONTROL

The site security or facility managers and restricted area owners are the second line of defense. They let your SOC know who should have access and at what level to their respected area whether its 24/7 or just Monday through Friday.

The SOC should never decide who gets access and who does not. It should be understood by all employees through company policy that the SOC programs access to a card only after requests are approved by the assigned authorized site or restricted area approvers. Default access makes the SOC's life easier and those of the site security managers involved. All screened and cleared employees and often contractors are entitled to default access at the site, state, or region where they work. For example, if someone works in one state and requests access to a site in another state, then where they are based you give him or her the Monday–Friday default access. Most new fulltime employees should automatically be given the area default they work in. If a person will be traveling between different sites or business units in different states, they can be automatically given that site default where they will travel too. Card access changes for any employee should only be made by that person's supervisor or manager and the site management or restricted area owners. Site directors, managers, and other supervisors can appoint a delegate title to one or more team individuals to be their main point-of-contact (POC) the SOC for access request, most often a team supervisor or even an executive administrator. Or these POC's main duty could be to act as the backup for authorizing access requests for when the primary person is out of town or on paid time off.

If an employee calls the SOC requesting access to a door they currently do not have authorization for at that time, the employee or contractor should be directed to submit an access request form to the SOC for proper processing and record-keeping. Card access requests can be made by e-mail from the supervisor to the SOC or directly to a SCO, but we strongly recommend that you discourage staff to email your SCOs directly because if they are on vacation then their request will sit there until the SCO returns. This happens when customers get used to working with a specific SCO, they tend to send their request to them directly. Your operators should try to encourage the customer when talking with or emailing the customer not to do this since that SCO may not always be on duty to complete the request. We recommend that you set up an access request form on your company's internal website usually on the security page that once completed is sent directly into the SOC group email box for any operator to be able to process quickly. The link should require people to add all of the information that the SOC will need to be able to promptly complete the access request.

SETTING UP AND CONTROLLING YOUR RESTRICTED AREAS ACCESS

RST areas are those places determined to be of a critical nature due to regulation, corporate policy, or by the manager and requires strict access control.

A restricted area could be a single room, multiple rooms, or an entire site. All your RST areas should be identified in your access control system by having "RST" at the end of the reader names and the access levels to differentiate them from the regular default access from a location.

CREATING A RESTRICTED AREA

Every restricted area needs an "owner" to be responsible for controlling the access to that location by authorizing and reviewing current access. The owner of a restricted area is usually someone who has authority over the functions located in the restricted area but can be anyone as designated by security or management personnel. There should be a minimum of at least two owners per restricted area but three or four would be preferred. Having multiple owners helps to ensure that there is always an owner available to complete access requests even when someone is on vacation or on business travel. When an area needs to be restricted an owner notifies the SOC they would like to restrict access to their area. The SOC should inform them to send the list of card access readers that will be part of that restricted access level and includes a list of all people authorized access to that area as well as the additional names as the co-owners. The owners are then the only people authorized to give permission for access into that area. Your SOC should maintain a restricted area owners list that includes the name of the restricted area and the owners of that area along with all their contact information. The list should be in a location either electronically or in a binder where all SCOs can easily gain access for review. The owners should receive a regular report at the interval of their choice such as a weekly, monthly, or quarterly report of all who have access to their RST area.

After creating the restricted area, the SOC should take the area out of the default access group and create a separate reader group solely for that area and putting an RST at the end of it. The SOC then assigns access to the people submitted on the list from the owners. However, there are sometimes exceptions to the rule for some areas such as executives, facilities, and security personnel. The owners should be made aware of such exceptions when applicable unless some form of regulation or corporate policy forbids such privileged access. They might also provide additional reasons why such personnel should not have access. The SOC then adds the area with the names of the owners onto the RST area owners list and their daytime contact info. Anytime a new restricted area is created, an email should go out to all of the SOC staff making them aware of the change. Once all of that work has been completed, the SOC should inform the owners that their area is now restricted and send them the final report of who has access to that area. The owner should also be notified that they may request from the SOC at any time, via email, additional reports listing those who have attempted access, those who have been granted access, and other access listings such as date and time. When an employee or contractor has been terminated, all of their RST access should be removed from their access card immediately and a new report sent to the area owners.

Access Approvals, Denials, and Removals

If an access request is for access to an area that is restricted, the requesting person should be directed to the owner of the access area for access approval if the owner requires a reason as to why the employee is requesting access to that area. Or the SOC can send the request directly to the owner for a yay or nay decision. The owner of the restricted area should notify the SOC in writing usually via email whether or not they give the requestor permission for access requested. The restricted areas and owners' names for each site should be located where SCOs can easily and quickly gain access for review like a shared drive folder or on a list posted within the SOC. Any changes requested by an owner should be accompanied by an email or an access request form for future document retention as proof of authorization. This protects your SOC from false accusations that they have given an individual access without owner approval. These requests should come to the SOC via email and intranet from personnel wanting access to that area or the owners themselves wanting to change someone's rights. Requests that are not from the owners should then be forwarded onto the primary owner and copy the backup to the owners for one of them to approve the request. A paper or electronic copy of the Approval/Denial/Removal Request will be saved and placed in the RST area file for future retention. Always follow up with the customer and/or owners via email when access has been added or denied by the owners. This shows the requestor that you are not the one deciding if they should or should not have access. Having a template removal email written into your post orders will help to ensure that customers understand.

REMOVAL Email Example

Subject line:Removal from a restricted area

To all [or individual name],

The SOC has been instructed to remove your access from [*name of RST area*] per the instructions of [*RST area owner name*] who is the owner of the area. If you feel that this is in error, or you still need to have access to the area,

If you have any further questions, please feel free to call the SOC at 555–555–5555 or email directly to: securityoperationscenter@company.com

We have a staff ready to assist you 24 hours a day, 7 days a week. We thank you for taking the time to look these over and working with us so closely. Have a great day!

[SCO signature block]

END OF Example

By highlighting that the requestor should contact the area owners, take the onus off of you and put the responsibility solely on the area owner for access control.

ACCESS CONTROL MATRIX

	A room is determined to be critical by its owner or due to regulation			
	↓			
	The owner notifies the SOC			
	↓			
	The owner submits a list of people authorized to have access	→	The list is sent to owners for review on a regular interval	
	↓			
	The owner submits 1−3 names as additional owners			
	↓			
	SOC takes readers out of default access and create RST access			
	↓			
	SOC assigns access to those on list provided by owners			
	↓			
	Personnel submit request to access of RST area through SOC			
	↓			
	SOC forwards request to owners for approval			
	↓			
Request is denied and customer notified.	NO	Approved?	YES	Requestor has RST area added to their access

SITE ACCESS CONTROL

Customers at sites may contact the SOC using such devices as telephones or their cell phones and even a site intercom to request access into a specific site or area. They could be calling from the elevator lobby of an office or from outside a gate at a plant. They might be calling from the site phone outside the main entrance because they forgot their access card, their access card doesn't have the proper access assigned to the card or to discuss site issues such as perimeter or closed area alarms that the SOC may monitor and control. When working with personnel onsite your operators do not normally work with it is important to verify the person they are speaking with is an actual employee or contractor for the company. They may try to plead their case for you to let them in but you should never grant access or discuss building details with anyone unless you can positively identify them. You should have a policy written for the SOC on what they should try to do for such calls. Below is an example of what you could write and train your SCOs to do in the event that such a call takes place:

Follow These Steps

1. Ask the person their name.
2. If they have their badge on their person, ask them to scan it again.
3. If that site has cameras you should try to pull the camera up at that site on that door and/or person and compare the badge picture to the person you see on the camera.
4. If that site has S/Os you should dispatch security to that position to investigate further.
5. If there are no cameras or S/Os, then check site procedures for any special instructions pertaining to that site and access.
6. If no special instructions, you should inform the customer that you are required to ask them a series of questions to verify they are who they say they are before you can proceed to help them. This is important to determine whether or not the person you are speaking to is actually an employee, or contractor.
7. Verify their employee ID number and ensure that they are in the PACS. Make sure they are still an active employee, or contractor.
8. Look the person up in the company directory. Utilize the information there to ask questions to help verify the identity of the individual. Ask questions such as:
9. Who is your manager?
10. What department are you in?
11. Which business group are you a part of?
12. What is your office phone number?

13. What company do you work for (if contractor)?
14. Ask them who the security or facility manager is for their site.
15. If at any time you believe they are who they say they are but are not sure if you should be discussing this issue with them, call the local site security or facility manager for authorization.
16. If they answer your questions correctly and you are sure the customer is who they say they are, you can grant access for that individual. Inform them you will now send a grant access command to the door.
17. Ask them to stay on the line with you until they get inside, if they are on a cell phone.
18. Ask them to ensure that the gate or door secures behind them.

In the event you grant access to a facility you must email the site security manager informing them of the situation and the actions you took. You should also make a DAR entry documenting any remote access you provided to any customer.

In the event that you deny access to someone at a facility you should write an IR documenting the denied remote access, with all actions taken and personnel notified. You must email the IR to the site security or facility manager informing them of the situation and the actions you took.

SYSTEM STATUS CHECKS

To ensure that your PACS is running properly and at an optimal level of functionality, your SOC needs to conduct a system status check every night during your midnight shift. What this does is allow you to identify and fix problems before they become major issues during the course of the work day. If your SOC finds that the PACS panels are down for one location and they report the problem to your IT department, they might discover that the network was down and IT can get the Internet connectivity returned before people begin reporting to work in the morning.

This responsibility should be a part of your midnight shifts daily duties and written in your post orders as such. The midnight shift should utilize your PACS panels and readers to check the current status each piece of equipment is currently communicating with the system and that the panel's firmware is currently up to date. Every problem should be documented in your DAR. SOC management will need to decide if you want your midnight staff to begin the troubleshooting process at the time of issue discovery by calling or notifying sites via email that their system does not status correctly or wait until the dayshift arrives for duty to let them deal with the problem. This is really a company preference. Some things can easily be done by your staff such as calling IT to ensure that Internet connectivity is good or perhaps restarting your PACS communications servers to reestablish communications. An email documenting the current status of the PACS should be sent to the SOC dayshift and copying security management letting them know what issues were discovered with the PACS and video systems. More on video in Chapter 11.

TROUBLESHOOTING

The most common troubleshooting call any SOC will receive is "my badge is not working on the door. Can you help me?" In our experience, we learned that many operators would follow different steps to check why a card might not be working, often missing some key steps and make a determination that a service call is needed without doing due diligence in trying to determine why a badge or card reader is not working. Vendors would show up at the site and discover the only problem was that the card was deactivated or the reader was in lock mode.

The following troubleshooting checklist was created with that purpose in mind to give operators a step-by-step process to check all of the common reasons why a badge or card reader might not be working. The main goal was to reduce the amount of services calls that are made to the vendor and save the company budget from unnecessary wasteful vendor trips and charges. This checklist can easily be modified to meet your company's needs and work within your various departments such as your companies network operations center.

HISTORICAL LESSONS

Access control can be very easy as shown in the access control matrix. The SCOs are the administrators of your enterprise PACS but only provide access to someone upon the authorization of the site and/or area owner or security management. Your procedures should state that the SCOs are not allowed to grant access without authorization and that such an action is a punishable offense. It is important that the SCOs never be responsible for deciding who should have access to a site or area only completing the access programming per management request. At companies where access control is not centralized, you will encounter security or facility managers that want to retain full access control over their site and loudly proclaim that they do not need a SOC to run their site. To earn their trust and keep them happy, provide them with as many reports of access that they want to show your staff is not tampering with the access they have authorized.

1. Is card ACTIVE?	YES	Go to step # 1.1
	NO	Investigate why? LOST? EXPIRED? TERMED? RETIRED?
1.1 Does the card have the correct access? Or Correct Pin if applicable?	YES	Go to step # 1.2
	NO	Go to step # 6 (If person traveling in different region, then grant that other region default access.)
1.2 Does the reader "Beep" when card is presented? Does it "beep" for others?	YES	Go to step # 2
	NO	Possible DEAD reader. Go to step # 2

| 2. Does the card work (beep or light change) at other readers? | YES | Possible strike or Mag lock issue. Ask which one the door has then Go to step # 3 |
| | NO | DEAD Card. Have customer request new badge. |

| 3. Can you status the reader? | YES | Go to step # 4 Make sure it is in the proper status |
| | NO | Go to step # 8 |

| 4. Can you send Lock/unlock Commands? Does the lock "Click"? | YES | Go to step # 5 |
| | NO | Go to step # 15 |

| 5. Current firmware? Download and Recheck – Has problem been fixed? | YES | Go to step # 6 |
| | NO | Go to step # Download at proper time and check again. |

| 6. Is the area restricted? | YES | Go to step # 7 |
| | NO | Go to step # 14 |

| 7. Does the Restricted Area Owner approve access? | YES | Add access and go to step # 14 |
| | NO | Contact requestor and inform them to contact the restricted area owner for access. |

| 8. Can you status the panel? | YES | Go to step # 14 |
| | NO | Go to step # 9 |

9. Can you ping the panel?	☐ YES	Go to step # 10
	☐ NO	Go to step # 12

10. Can you ping the Video at the site (if applicable)	☐ YES	Go to step # 17
	☐ NO	Go to step # 11

11. Are you able to Trace route to the site?	☐ YES	Go to step # 12
	☐ NO	Go to step # 13

12. Check same PACS server for other sites having issues if so, reboot. Did this solve the problem?	☐ YES	Go to step # 28
	☐ NO	Go to step # 13

13. Possible network problem. Call IT. Did this resolve the issue?	☐ YES	Go to step # 28
	☐ NO	Go to step # 17

14. GIVE PROPER ACCESS – Go to step # 28

15. SERVICE CALL – Possible Strike or electrical problem, Set up Work Order and go to Step # 18   (NOTE: IF THIS INVOLVES A GATE – REFER TO STEP #18.1 then Jump to Step 29)

16. SERVICE CALL – Possible Bad Reader or other problem, Set up Work Order and go to Step #18

17. SERVICE CALL – Possible Bad Panel- Set up Work Order and go to Step # 18

18. Determine Which Vendor this is to be assigned to.			

18.1 – You may need to coordinate with Vendor, facilities, and/or responsible Physical Security Specialist to arrange a meeting date and time for all 3 to be on-site to fix problem.

19. PRIORITY LEVEL Contact Security Management for Priority Level Determination Dayshift. – If unable to contact someone – still do steps 20-28. But <u>DO NOT</u> call vendor!!	#1 ☐	#2 ☐	#3 ☐	#4 ☐
Level Determination Made by:				

20. START WORK ORDER PROCESS (Follow steps #21 - #26 in order) Consult Post Orders for more detailed Info	
21. Click on "Work Order" in the ticket System.	☐ (Check when completed)
22. Enter in site information.	☐ (Check when completed)

23. Enter in detail information of the problem in Notes Section.	☐ (Check when completed)
24. Enter in Site Contact Name and Telephone #.	☐ (Check when completed)
25. Enter in Alternate Site Contact Name and Telephone #.	☐ (Check when completed)
26. Select SOC and click "Dispatch" to dispatch WO to SOC Email.	☐ (Check when completed)
27. Once #21-#26 are completed, go to step #28.	

28. FOLLOW UP WITH CUSTOMER WITH THE CURRENT STATUS OF THE REQUEST!

GATE TROUBLESHOOTING INSTRUCTIONS
(For Sites that state a gate isn't working properly)

29. Is the power on to the gate controller?	☐ YES	Go to step # 30
	☐ NO	Turn on power, go to step # 36

30. Is the gate on the rolling track?	☐ YES	Go to step # 31
	☐ NO	Go to step # 38

31. Is there anything in front of the anti-crush safety sensor?	☐ YES	Remove the item, go to step # 37
	☐ NO	Go to step # 32

32. Is there anything that could physically prevent the gate from closing? (ICE, snow, rocks, branches, tumbleweeds, etc.)	☐ YES	Remove item, go to step #37
	☐ NO	Go to step # 33

33. Does the gate's drive chain appear to be broken?	☐ YES	Go to step # 37
	☐ NO	Go to step # 34

34. If the gate isn't opening or closing all of the way, does the gate stop at the same location?	☐ YES	Go to step # 37
	☐ NO	Go to step # 37

| 35. Has the manual override switch engaged? Place back to "Aux". SOC sends lock, unlock, and lock commands. Have person run their card at the reader. Is the gate moving?? | ☐ YES | Go to step # 39 |
| | ☐ NO | Go to step # 36 |

| 36. Turn off power for 15 seconds, and then turn power back on. SOC sends lock, unlock, and lock commands. Is the gate now moving?? | ☐ YES | Go to step # 39 |
| | ☐ NO | Go to step # 38 |

| 37. Have person run his/her card at the gate readers and SOC sends lock, unlock, and lock commands. Is the gate now moving??? | ☐ YES | Go to step # 39 |
| | ☐ NO | Go to step # 38 |

38. Re-engage the manual override and pull gate shut. SOC – Set up service call and give WO# to reporting party. Go to steps # 21- 26

39. Gate is now properly working again per confirmation of site personnel. Make note in DAR and send email to Dayshift SCO's, SOC Manager and Corporate Security Personnel.

At one company, in the early days of setting up a brand new SOC, one site security manager had full admin access to the PACS. He took away all the SCO's ability to make any changes to his location without telling anyone. A short time later, a different employee was terminated from the company at the end of the day and extremely upset over the termination. The termed employee left the site very angry. After the employee drove away, the human resources person realized they forgot to collect the termed employee's access card. Frantic, she quickly went to the security manager's office only to learn that he had left for the day. The HR manager called the security managers cell phone only to find it going right to voicemail. She left several messages. The security manager lived well over an hour's drive away from the work location and Friday afternoons were the worst drive of the week. When he got home the security manager discovered that his cell phone had died, so he plugged it into charge. That's when he learned he had several messages and called the HR manager back immediately. She was angry he was not reachable, he was angry she had not informed him of the termination prior to the termination. She explained that the termed employee was very upset when he left and she was afraid he might try to come back that night or over the weekend. The security manager left his laptop at work so he knew he would have to drive all the way back in through rush hour just to deactivate a badge. Then he thought "hey, I'll call that new SOC they built at corporate." The security manager called the SOC only to learn that the SCOs were not able to help him. The call went something like this:

"Why the hell not?! I thought that's what you guys were there for?" said the security manager in a frantic tone due to the heat he was catching from HR for being unreachable.

"I'm sorry sir, we seem to have lost access to make changes to your site" said the SCO.

"How is that possible?!" said the security manager angrily.

"I'm not sure sir, let me run a report" said the SCO and followed up with "sir the report shows that you took away our access a couple of weeks ago."

"Oh. Yeah. . . . . I forgot" said the security manager. In a sheepish and new friendly tone, he said "is there anything we can do? I really don't want to have to drive home."

The SOC called Jarpey who could log in remotely from home. Jarpey was a full admin too and could quickly fix the SCO's access who then deactivated the termed employee's card with instructions to create an alarm if the card is used over the course of the weekend. The security manager was informed that the access card was deactivated and they would notify him if an attempt at access was made by the termed employee. To which he replied "Huh?! I guess this SOC thing really works."

CHAPTER 10

Alarm Monitoring

INTRODUCTION

Your SOC will be monitoring alarms through your PACS through network servers, a burglar alarm system through alarm signal receivers or in some cases your SOC may use both systems side by side depending upon the monitoring requirement. Your staff is responsible for assessing and responding to those alarm signals they electronically receive through the various systems your SOC utilizes to secure the perimeter of critical areas within your company's locations. The purpose of this chapter is to provide a basic guideline for handling the alarms your SOC will monitor.

PHYSICAL ACCESS CONTROL SYSTEM (PACS) OR INTRUSION DETECTION SYSTEM (IDS) ALARMS

We believe that the best alarm monitoring system with a PACS or intrusion detection system (IDS) is one that works hand-in-hand with a video surveillance system and is the standard we have promoted within our companies that we have worked for. The reason for this standard is that video allows your SOC to verify whether or not an alarm is real or false. More law enforcement agencies are refusing to respond to alarm calls if the dispatching station cannot confirm they have video or audio confirmation of some form of unauthorized activity taking place at the location. Or if they do respond and find that the alarm call was false, they will charge your company anywhere from $50 to $300 or more just for the service they performed by responding. With video surveillance, if your SOC receives an alarm they can quickly review the video from the site in which the alarm was received to determine if the alarm is valid. If there is video proof that unauthorized activity is taking place such as a break-in, your SOC will receive a faster response from local law enforcement if they can tell the 911 dispatcher that they have unauthorized activity on camera and are able to describe the individuals involved.

Security Operations Center Guidebook. DOI: http://dx.doi.org/10.1016/B978-0-12-803657-0.00010-6

ALARM INSTRUCTIONS

As the SOC manager you will need to determine what the basic standard of alarm response is for each alarm across the company and incorporate that into your site procedures. Most door forced and door held open alarms can be easily written to be processed in a standard step-by-step process but every company is different and many alarms within your company may have more criticality or importance than others. When you have a door or doors to a room that require specialized actions, these instructions should be written into your PACS for quick review by your SOC staff when working with these types of alarms. Training your staff to process alarms the same way every time an alarm is received will help to ensure that your staff makes it a regular habit versus being unsure or confused. You must create instructions in your equipment procedures using screenshots for training purposes showing step-by-step actions in how to open an alarm and close an alarm from the monitoring queue.

RECEIVING ALARMS

Upon receiving a door forced, door held open, or other type of alarms, SCOs should open the alarm in the alarm monitoring panel, check for special instructions written in the system, and then acknowledge the alarm to silence the audible alarm.

HOW AN ALARM IS HANDLED DEPENDS ON THE THREE STEPS OF ASSESSMENT

Assessment of an alarm is the most crucial step in alarm processing in order to respond correctly. The first part of assessment is to determine what type of alarm it is as previously stated. In many cases, a monitor point in alarm is more serious than a door held open or door forced.

1. First step is to determine what type of alarm that you have received. A door forced is a contact alarm that take places when the door is opened without proper card access authorization such as a break-in or someone using a key to override the lock. This can happen if the door is not secured properly and it is simply pushed or pulled open. It can also happen if the employee uses a key on the door instead of an access card. A monitor point in alarm is a motion, glass break, or a similar type of alarm. Door held open alarms are either the door was held open a little longer than the time designated within the reader settings or the door is stuck open. Always check the status of the door to make sure it closed properly.

2. Second step is to determine where the alarm is coming from and if it is an exterior, interior, or restricted area door. All alarms should be clearly written so that each SCO can easily understand what the alarm is and their criticality.
3. Third step is to verify at what time and date did the alarm occur, which needs to be assessed. This is important in determining because if it is a late alarm coming in due to loss of connectivity between the panel and the server or if the alarm going off is in the present tense. Network outages happen often and for various amounts of time. A late alarm receipt may require different assessment actions altogether depending upon the gap of time involved such as calling the police immediately to investigate and sending the site security manager to meet the police.

RESPONSE

As soon as the alarm is assessed there should be a response that is required by your SOC staff. General response for most alarm activity is to first check the card access activity history report at the location to see if there is valid card activity at the site to determine if people are on site, then checking the status of the other equipment such as the doors and gates to see if other issues are present that raise concern. How the alarm is handled further may depend on the specific site procedure for the location where the alarm is occurring. If video surveillance is available at the location a review of current active video for the entire site and checking the camera that pertains to the door or area that is in alarm. The following are two examples that could be used in your site procedures for alarm assessment pertaining to a site with and without security officers on site.

Response for Alarms for Sites with Security Officers

1. Contact the site security officer via phone to have him or her investigate the cause of the alarm. Note: If security patrol officer does not respond after two attempts, then contact the alternate on site security personnel if applicable.
2. Check current access card activity to determine if an employee is working onsite and may have set off the alarm.
3. Check the cameras at the site, if available, for any suspicious behavior or activity.
4. If the security officer reports that the area is secure, note that in the comments section of the alarm acknowledge window, then skip to step 9. If the security officer reports questionable activity in the area and asks the SOC to visually monitor, confirm visual contact with site security on the call and move to next step.

5. If site security determines that there is an unauthorized individual in the area or a break-in has occurred, call the police.
6. Inform the security officer to observe the individual(s) while staying at a safe distance or, if they are already gone, have the security officer secure the perimeter from any further unauthorized access until the police arrive.
7. Once incident resolution has occurred, ensure that the security officer completes an IR and notifies the site safety and security manager, contacts of the incident along with any other appropriate personnel.
8. Any damage to the building, which affects perimeter security or presents a safety hazard to personnel needs to be reported to facilities personnel from the call list immediately.
9. Write down the time of dispatch and descriptions of all activity in the DAR.
10. Contact the site security management or your SOC chain of command with any questions.

Alarms for Sites with No Guards

1. Check the cameras (if applicable) at the site for any suspicious behavior or activity. If yes, skip to step 5. If valid employee activity through the video surveillance system is recorded, skip to step 3. If unsure move to the next step.
2. Check current access card activity to determine if there is valid card activity onsite and an employee may have inadvertently set off the alarm. If yes, move to step 3. If unsure, skip to step 4.
3. If there is valid employee activity, acknowledge and note that in the comments section in the alarm and skip to step 9.
4. Using the most recent badge access info, attempt to contact a person who has most recently used their badge at the site. If contact is made, ask if they are the ones who may have set off the alarm and/or could check the area in question or close a door held open, such as the door they may have come through and caused a door held open alarm. If the contacted employee observes an unknown person in the area, tell them to get to a safe place and call the police.
5. If the determination is made that an unauthorized individual is in the area or a break-in has occurred, the SOC should also notify the police. Then notify the site security contact.
6. Continue to monitor and document situation as it unfolds.
7. Complete an IR and send a copy of the report to the site safety and security manager contacts.
8. Any damage to the building, which affects perimeter security or presents a safety hazard to personnel needs to be reported to facilities personnel from the call list immediately.

9. Write all activity in the DAR.
10. Contact the site or your SOC chain of command with any questions.

MECHANICAL ALARMS

A mechanical alarm is often associated with different types of equipment such as boilers, storage tanks, refrigeration equipment, and various similar items. Mechanical alarms could include but are not limited to:

- Temperature out of acceptable range.
- Equipment malfunction.
- Water leakage.

When a mechanical alarm is received in your PACS, a special or unique audio notification should be designated to differentiate the alarm from regular intrusion-related alarms. The sound chosen should be dependent upon the severity or importance of the alarm. A high temperature alarm for a refrigeration unit that is keeping valuable and expensive equipment cool may need a different level of response to a water leak alarm. These types of alarms still require a response but the actions will most likely include notification of onsite or offsite personnel and should be noted in your site procedures.

PANIC ALARMS

These will have a more urgent nature and will most likely require an immediate dispatch of security or law enforcement personnel. A panic alarm at most companies involves a receptionist at the main entrance of a building or an alarm in a parking lot or structure. Panic alarms mean that someone feel they are under imminent threat of danger and they need help. We cannot stress enough that you must have a quick response ready for these types of alarms, along with a solid action plan and procedure in place for each panic alarm before they are installed. If you do not, you run the risk of exposing your SOC to failure that could result in serious injury or the loss of life. Obviously, that is something you want to avoid at all costs.

REDUCE YOUR FALSE ALARMS

Most the alarms received by your SOC will be false. This is a fact affirmed by everyone we've spoken to across the security industry. There are several different reasons for this to include improper programming of the information into the software systems, incorrect installation of the hardware to the panels, and more often because of the actions of the personnel at the locations. They'll prop doors open, use keys to bypass the PACS or completely sabotage the system by duct taping over the strikes or using magnets to disrupt the mag locks. The list is endless and many of us could easily commiserate for hours on the different ways our employees have succeeded in bypassing the access control system. But constant false alarms are dangerous to your SOC.

False alarms will breed complacency in your entire SOC staff. If you do not take regular action and steps to reduce the amount of false alarms within your systems, then you run the risk of missing a real alarm that required action and any failure on the part of your staff will reflect upon the entire operation and the entire corporate security department. Mistakes lead management personnel to wonder what they are paying for if people are missing alarms that results in company losses and they'll begin to wonder if the money being spent should not be outsourced to a third-party vendor. These are some steps you can take to reduce the false alarms within your system.

1. Check with your SOC staff and facility personnel
   a. Unless you are a SOC manager or supervisor who sits post on a regular basis after hours, you are not going to know how bad the false alarms are within your system. The majority of false alarms do not start popping up in the system until well after the regular work day is done. Most operators are not going to inform you how bad the false alarms are without asking because they do not want to "rock the boat" so you need to take the first step. You need to spend some time with your staff while on after-hour shifts and ask them how bad the false alarms are and once you do, be prepared to take notes because they will be more than willing to inform you how ridiculous they think the amount of false alarms they receive is during their shift.
   b. Ask them to identify the top 5 or 10 locations within your system with false alarms.
   c. Then ask them the 5 or 10 most common repeated alarms from those locations. They will know and they will be able to provide you with a list that you can begin to work from.
   d. If an alarm has become a regular problem suddenly it may be due to increased work at the site and employees are working later for whatever reason or a new shift has been added. Send an alarm history report to local site security management and ask them if there is a reason for these alarms to be increasing. You just might learn that the site has added an evening shift and forgot to tell you.
2. Work on one site at a time
   a. Prioritize the list with the worst-cited location being the first priority of reducing the amount of false alarms received. If it is

within your company's budget, it is strongly recommended that the SOC manager should be allowed to travel to these locations that are having issues. It is our belief that every SOC will benefit extremely when the SOC manager has visited each site within their system and met personally with local management.

b. Determine the hours of operation at that facility and work with the site security contact to determine which alarms can be bypassed during the day. If people are working onsite, there is no need for door held open alarms to come into your SOC, because employees are standing in the doorway holding the door open and talking with each other while taking a smoke break. Remember it is not always just dayshift that needs to be bypassed. If you have a facility with a second or third shift working onsite, then you will need to determine what are the critical alarms that still need to report into your SOC during those shifts, and that is accomplished by working through your corporate security staff or site security or management personnel.

c. Create alarm bypass commands within your system that will prevent those alarms from reporting during the sites hours of operations.

d. Be very careful when programming to ensure that you or your staff did not accidentally add a panic or other important alarm that should continue to be monitored into the bypass command that you create to void out alarms.

e. Conduct training with personnel at the site being monitored. You can do this by holding lunch and learn presentations that talk about security and why it is important to make sure your employees shut the door behind them when they enter the site. Train them to call the SOC when they enter a site after hours and weekends.

f. Post signage on at the various site entrances that have the phone number to your SOC and state what to do when entering and exiting the facility after hours.

g. Check with your vendor to ensure that the intrusion detection equipment actually works. We will discuss this more in Chapter 12.

3. Review and test:

4. a. You have completed the original list and hopefully your SOC has seen a massive reduction in false alarms but you will learn they never go away. NEVER. They will continue to come in because of employee mistakes, employee subversion, or faulty hardware and equipment.

b. You must continually review with your team and encourage your staff to report runaway alarms that need fixing such as a bad door contact that keeps sending a door into alarm even though the door is in the closed position.

    c. Work with local or field personnel. Have your local site personnel such as security or facility manager test the system for potential or visible issues that your people are starting to notice in the alarm monitoring system. Train your staff that they are owners of your systems and it is up to them to make sure everything works well.

    d. Make it a regular habit to ensure that the reduction of false alarms is an ongoing process. This will only serve to ensure that your staff does not become complacent.

HISTORICAL LESSONS

Anyone reading this book who knows anything about alarm monitoring knows that false alarms are the bane of any SOC. They are always going to happen due to hardware or software issues but primarily because of the human element. At one company, there was a rear door on a site that had a mag lock on the door that was used by employees to enter the work location after they parked within the perimeter. This is one of the few doors that did not have a video camera pointed at it because management decided they didn't want employees to think they were being watched all the time. It was a site that usually had people working round the clock.

Over the course of one weekend the SOC kept getting "Door Forced" alarms for that door. The SCOs knew that people were working and called some folks at the site who said the door is just fine. The SOC called the facility manager who said she'd look at it when she returns to work. Monday morning the site facility manager came in at 6am to discover that the door could be pulled open without scanning her access card. She called the SOC who said they received another door forced alarm, attempted to troubleshoot the issue with her, but ultimately had to put in a ticket for service. The vendor came out and within 2 minutes the door was restored and functioning properly. This same event went on 4 days in a row. On the fifth day, the service technician said, "Look this is getting ridiculous. Tell the managers here that someone keeps putting magnets in between the mag locks. That's why it's not securing." It was later discovered that the overnight crews were tampering with the lock to freely go in and out for additional breaks and not have to scan back into the building. Approximately 2 weeks later, a video camera was added to that door.

CHAPTER 11

Enterprise Video Surveillance

INTRODUCTION

Video surveillance should be just as necessary to your SOC as access control. They work best together but video can also work without a PACS alarm system due to motion alarms within video systems. With video, you can "see" what is happening on site. With an alarm in your PACS all you know is that your SOC has received a door held open alarm. By looking at the camera pointed at the door the alarm came in you can see why the door is held open by playing back the video from the last 30 seconds or more and make a quick determination whether it was an actionable alarm that requires dispatch of response. Most likely your SOC staff will see an employee who held the door open too long or that the door did not shut all the way after an employee entered or exited that doorway. Without video, all you know is that there is a door held open alarm, which might mean a burglar has propped that door open while they begin to haul your company's property out of the building.

We strongly recommend that your SOC utilize only one VMS platform and that it be a corporate policy to ensure that your sites do not take it upon themselves to put in their "own" system. It is difficult for operators to effectively use multiple VMS platforms in a SOC at the same time. It creates unnecessary extra work for your staff by having to jump from one platform to the next. This could cause a problem if they need to pull up a certain camera quickly due to a site emergency or alarm received and they open the wrong platform because they are managing several different projects at one time.

Your operators should be taught that they are the eyes of the corporate security department. Just like security officers, the SOC operators have the responsibility to "observe and report" all discrepancies they observe while monitoring video, then take the appropriate actions as directed by company procedure or policy.

Security Operations Center Guidebook. DOI: http://dx.doi.org/10.1016/B978-0-12-803657-0.00011-8

OPERATOR PERMISSIONS

Just like with your PACS, the SOC staff should not all have the same permissions within the VMS until each individual operator has proven that they can properly handle such tasks as programming a new camera or modifying an existing one without damaging existing system programming. Giving a new SOC operator higher permissions in the VMS system to change a camera name or preset when they do not have the proper experience is again asking for problems that you do not need to happen. Create levels that each operator must works toward achieving for gaining new system permissions within your VMS. Whether an operator receives higher permissions within the VMS usually depends on the operator's skills and their capabilities as they learn the system. A simple way to set up the access permissions is creating different levels that can be assigned as your operators prove themselves capable. Each VMS user interface is different and you must select what levels are best for your SOC, such as:

1. *SCO Level I*—Live + Search which means they can view video and replay video.
2. *SCO Level II*—This level adds the ability to archive video for posterity.
3. *SCO Level III*—This level adds the ability to create new sites or cameras and other items in the VMS.
4. *ADMIN*—This permission level should be reserved for the most trusted of personnel and management.

You have to be sure to define what these levels are and what the SCOs need to do to get to the next level. A good way to ensure that your SCOs continue to work to the next level in either or both of your PACS and VMS is make it clear that when they accomplish the necessary actions to increase their skills to achieve the next level of access that they will earn a small pay increase.

SETTING UP YOUR VIDEO MONITORING SYSTEM

Companies that utilize a corporate-wide enterprise VMS must ensure that the chosen software platform and camera brands are compatible with your company operating system standards and your network. Your IT department should be a part of the decision-making process and a project manager ought to be assigned to consult and provide help where needed to ensure a smooth transition. Fortunately, many of the available VMS software brands on the market now allow for recording video at a higher level at the edge to the local recorder or server on site and then streaming across the network at a lower level to reduce the amount of bandwidth being used by a monitoring station in your SOC.

There are many different brands of cameras and each one is different from the other. Still cameras should be pointed at the area or object that it is protecting. Interior cameras views should not have the clear majority of a picture view looking at the ceiling of the facility. Exterior cameras should avoid having landscape views that primarily capture the sky or an area unimportant to the areas being monitored by the VMS. Each camera with pan, tilt, zoom (PTZ) capabilities should have at least three presets programmed into them that focus on the most important areas that may need to be checked on a regular or rotating basis.

Your SOC should have a wall of monitors that is primarily used for video monitoring. In the past, we have used PCs with powerful video cards, high-quality HDMI cables, and KVM switches so that with one keyboard and mouse, operators could control one PC right at the workstations, and another one connected to the wall monitors displaying video, which is one of the easiest and cheapest methods. If your company has a larger budget, there are many other different forms of video wall monitoring systems that could be purchased to be programmed and controlled directly at the operator's workstation. The goal is to have your most crucial areas under constant observation. Your SOC might have more sites or important areas to monitor than video wall space available, so you may have to set your VMS to rotate through cameras on a regular basis. If that is the case, then you should ensure that your system can do such a task automatically for you. When setting up your video wall in regard to the workstations, you must think about line-of-sight and distance from the workstation. The optimal video wall set up is to have the video wall be visible just above the workstation monitors, so all that an operator has to do is lift their eyes to glance at the video wall for anything of a suspicious or concerning nature and then go right back to performing their other duties on the workstation monitors.

Think about presentation when setting up your camera views and video wall. What goes on your wall? News? Weather? Map of your locations? What are the size of your camera views? What will a visitor or a VIP member of the chain-of-command think when they tour your SOC? You want everything on the wall to be of value to the primary mission of operator's duties to protect the company and its personnel but also impressive to visitors such as the C-suite of the executive staff. Every inch of your video wall should be utilized to show something of value and your staff should not have wasted space on their monitors. The cameras that are presented on the wall should have a specific value-added meaning or a particular reason for being on the wall because not all of your company's cameras will be able to fit. You need to think about the size of camera view on the video wall. If you cram as many cameras as you can on the wall and the views are so small that your staff cannot even tell what is going on inside that view or even what site the camera view is, then you have overloaded the amount of camera views on the wall. Operators should be able to quickly glance at a camera view and can tell what is happening within that picture and know exactly which site they are looking at. Just because your video wall does not put every camera on display this does not mean those cameras are not being used. That is when your remote video patrols are conducted.

REMOTE VIDEO PATROL

Security officers perform rounds during their shift. Depending on the size of the site or building, security officers will perform an average of two to three rounds per shift. This action should be no different for your SOC staff. Depending upon the number of sites and cameras you have across your VMS, the SOC staff should complete a minimum of two complete remote video patrols of every location every 4 hours. The frequency should be written into your SOC post orders. Areas that have been identified as high risk or targeted areas should be patrolled even more if they are not already posted on your video wall.

At each site that your SOC is responsible for monitoring video, the cameras should be opened in the VMS and every camera should be checked to ensure that all doors and gates are closed, and the SCOs should be looking for any other unusual conditions that would need to be reported quickly to the proper personnel. Some issues could just be written up in an incident report and sent out via email to the proper personnel for handling on the next business day. What purpose does this remote video patrol serve? Below are examples of what your staff could see while conducting a remote video patrol:

- Water leaks due to heavy rain, burst pipes, or toilets overflowing.
- Damage to facility due to natural disaster such as weather for earthquake.
- Door propped open and door contact tampered with.
- Safety hazards such as emergency exits blocked with supplies on palettes or other large pieces of equipment that would prevent someone trying to exit a building during an emergency.
- Employees using a door without using their access card because the strike was duct-taped and the door contact tampered with to prevent sending a door forced alarm.
- Smoke coming from coffee pots left on.
- Smoke coming from servers in data centers.
- Smoke coming from backup generators, and many other possibilities from items that create heat and friction.
- Employees or contractors stealing, sleeping on the job, or using drugs and/or alcohol among many other transgressions.

- Signs of vandalism such as spray painting on exterior walls or cracked or broken windows.
- Trespassers on property with intent to steal, or vandalize from the building, storage containers, company vehicles, or supplies stored out in the open within the company yard.
- Trespassers on property just to use the space to party.
- Trespassers parking on the property for a quickie in the parking lot.

All the previous examples may seem over the top but they are actual incidents that we have seen happen over the course of our many years' experience. Remote video patrols are most important for afterhours, weekends, and holidays when a site is mostly, if not completely, empty. By noticing a water leak on the floor of a building on a Saturday afternoon, a SOC operator could alert facilities personnel to respond and hopefully prevent the problem from becoming worse had they not seen or reported the issue, then facilities can work to get the problem resolved and possibly cleaned up before employees report back to work the next business day.

ALARM RESPONSE

Your VMS should work closely with your alarm monitoring system. If there is a perimeter door your SOC monitors, then there should always be a camera pointing at that same door. Upon receiving an alarm from your alarm monitoring system, the first step for your SOC after that alarm sounds should always be reviewing the camera video from the area of the alarm received to verify if the alarm is an actual alarm or false. Video verification that an alarm is valid is often necessary in many cities to get a fast and timely response from law enforcement officers and many law enforcement agencies will charge you a fee for responding to a false alarm at your location. Several will raise the fee higher and higher as the number of false alarm dispatches increase. Verifying an alarm through your VMS will help to reduce law enforcement dispatch to your location for a false alarm. This provides several benefits to include getting a reputation as a company that does not dispatch for false alarms, saves money because you will not be fined for false alarm response and local law enforcement will respond quickly when they are informed that you have witnessed something on your VMS.

INVESTIGATIVE SUPPORT

When something bad happens your SOC will be asked to review video. Video review requests may come from internal security personnel, internal audit, ethics compliance, HR, or other departments within your organization.

This is a service that provides value to your SOC when these other departments know they can rely on your SOC and their staff to provide that support and keep the information confidential.

Video review comes with the job and your staff must be given the proper guidance of what exactly they are looking for. Procedures should be in place on who is authorized to request review of video. That procedure could be as simple as "all video review requests must be sent to the SOC manager or the chain-of-command for approval." The reviewing of video has greater benefits other than watching for bad guys or reviewing for security reasons. More companies are using video surveillance for safety assurance and quality production control. Cameras watching a production line can be reviewed for employee performance and ensuring that they are following proper safety protocols. Regardless of what the reason is for video review, your SOC will be busy if you have multiple locations and hundreds of cameras. Some of the after-incident review requests we have received over the years are:

- Verify when an employee actually enters and/or leaves the building.
- Check to see if someone left the building with a piece of company property without company approval such as a computer or other piece of equipment.
- Review of employee's actions in an area under video surveillance.
- Damage to building or property due to vandalism or another incident.
- Parking lot damage to someone's vehicle.
- Review of accidents on productions lines.
- Review of actions taken by staff during an emergency such as a fire or mechanical failure.

CIVIL DISTURBANCE: STRIKES, PROTESTS, OR DEMONSTRATIONS

If your company is subject to any of the above possible actions, your SOC should have a procedure in place of what to do to include actions taken with your VMS. You'll want your SCOs to point as many available cameras as possible at the disturbance to capture as much of the action as possible. Paying special attention to such things as:

- Signs or banners advocating violence.
- Weapons or items that could possibly be used as weapons.
- Acts of violence.
- Acts of vandalism or other destruction of property.
- Leaders of the disturbance who appear to be advocating for violence and destruction.

The captured video will help law enforcement officials with their investigation into any violent or destructive actions that were taken.

DAILY SYSTEM STATUS CHECKS

Your SOC staff should understand that they are responsible for ensuring that all video equipment is operational and working to the best of its ability. Conducting daily system status checks on your VMS and reporting issues to SOC and/or site management are important to the success of the SOC. The last thing you want is to receive a request to review video from a certain camera and then you have to explain to that site customer the camera is down. Most people will ask you how long it has been down, if the answer is not to their liking.

As with your PACS system status checks, your staff should review every single camera within your VMS looking for problems such as:

- Video loss due to no signal or camera dying.
- Signs of tampering such as taped over, spray painted, pointed in a direction that serves no purpose such as directly at a wall or pointed toward the ground, and so on.
- Out of focus.
- Discoloring—usually a sign that an Internet Protocol (IP) camera is beginning to die.
- PTZ will not respond to commands to move.
- A piece of equipment has been placed in front of the camera that blocks the camera from seeing its intended area.

Any issue discovered should be documented in the DAR. This should include what the nature of the problem or issue found is, what troubleshooting actions the SCOs have taken to correct the issues, and the resolution if any. An email should be sent to the person at the site in charge of the VMS letting them know exactly what was discovered and what they did to try and fix the problem. The fact that your SOC could not correct the problem means the site needs to take an action such as moving the piece of equipment or placing a service call to the vendor.

HISTORICAL LESSONS

To integrate or not to integrate your VMS with your PACS, that is the question. We get asked that and the answer is truly "what works best for you?" We have not. The main factor in that decision is if for some reason, you lose your PACS and alarms, you will also lose your video. But if they are separated, at least you still have one or the other to fall back on to monitor your locations. "But if the PACS fails you could just go back to the VMS software" you say. True. But how well will your SOC staff be able to utilize that VMS software if they are not using the product for every shift they work? They might not be as efficient as they normally are in working with your VMS. If you have total faith in your Internet connection and confident that 90%–100% of the time you will stay online then by all means integrate your cameras into your PACS.

One of the most often asked questions about a SOC is "should I put video cameras in my SOC?" We always quickly reply "yes." The reason for that is if you have two people that perhaps do not get along personally working side by side for 8–12 hours, there may come a time when one SCO will accuse the other of wrongdoing. Cameras with microphones will help prevent that from happening or at the least quickly prove or disprove the accusation. The first time we put cameras in a SOC one of our more trusted, experienced, and dependable SCOs became very upset and confrontational stating loudly, "I guess there is no more trust around here!" The funny thing is now that same SCO is a SOC manager and utilizes the cameras in his SOC quite frequently to review what took place during the afterhours shifts. He admits this freely.

With video, you will see things you do not want to see that will leave you very disappointed in the people you work with and at other times you will get some great laughs. Many, many years ago, during a holiday and the office was closed, football was on the minds of many Americans for that day. Including one SCO who was working day shift with the lead SCO. The SOC manager was at home with their family and called into the SOC to talk to the lead SCO to see if everything was going okay. As the two were talking, the lead SCO burst into uncontrollable laughter so much so that they had to apologize and call back later. It went something like this, "BWAH-HAH-HAH-HAH-HA!!! OH, MY GOD!! BWAH-HAH-HAH-HAH-HA!! OH, MY GOD!! I'M SORRY!! I GOTTA CALL YOU BACK!!" Click. When the lead SCO finally gained control of their hysterical emotions and called back, the rest of the story was told. While talking with the SOC manager, the lead SCO was watching their shift partner return from a restroom break on the SOC main entrance video camera. The lead SCO watched as the other SCO on duty got into full football mode as the SCO positioned himself in front of the SOC entrance in a defensive lineman stance ready to rush the door upon entry. The SCO scanned his access card on the door entry reader but instead of waiting for the ball to snap, or rather the strike to click and grant access, the SCO rushed the door. The result, he firmly planted his bespectacled face and body on the door and was beaten back from the line of scrimmage quite handily. The door won the day on the line. Thus, began the laughter. This video was of course saved for posterity, shared with several, viewed hundreds of times, and used for training purposes on the importance of waiting for the strike to click and what NOT to do when entering a card reader door.

CHAPTER 12

Working with Your Vendors

INTRODUCTION

This chapter is about how your company should work with your national account vendor or local site vendors and how they work with your SOC. Many larger companies will work with one primary security integrator that will manage their account nationally and/or globally by using local branches or subcontractors to support your company locations. Regardless of how many vendors you use for security installations and service work, you should work with your supply chain and each of your selected vendors to create a company requirements document to go along with your SLA or master services agreement (MSA) for your vendors to understand your expectations for new installations and service work and how they relate to your SOC. This document is just as important to the vendor as it is to your company because their local branches need to be given a copy of the document for them to read and adhere to. The requirements document is important because it is primarily for the local vendors benefit to help ensure that they meet your expectations and properly complete their work in relation to your SOC. This writing will focus on one primary national account with a vendor that provides services to each location using their local branches.

SCOPE OF WORK

The first section should be about the scope of work that would be required with a new installation, retrofits, conversions, and service request work, and should explain the MSA you have in place with your vendor so their local branches understand that your local site is part of a national account and subject to discounted prices for products and services. This section could be detailed or simply introductory for the sake of the local vendor branch and include high-level contracted service items such as:

- [Company] maintains a 2-hour service response requirement for fire alarm systems.
- [Company] maintains a 4-hour service response requirement for IDSs.

113

Security Operations Center Guidebook. DOI: http://dx.doi.org/10.1016/B978-0-12-803657-0.00012-X

- All new sales, retrofits, or conversions for each branch must go through vendor's national accounts manager.
- Each new installation will be managed by vendor's national accounts project manager.
- All general security and integrated security solutions are monitored centrally through [Company]'s SOC located at their corporate office and all branches must work directly with their SOC to ensure proper completion of new installations and service requests.
- All system programming for the PACS and VMS will be completed by the [Company] SOC.
- Completion of service and repair requests for [Company] must be reported to vendors assigned national account and project manager.

YOUR COMPANY PROFILE

The "Client Profile" section is important because it is primarily for the vendors benefit of understating who your company is and how far it reaches. This section should include two detailed paragraphs. One about your company and the other about your SOC. The company paragraph should detail what kind of company you are and the various business units or subsidiaries within your company and the products or services you produce. Much like you would find on your company's website for the public to view. The more important paragraph is introducing the local vendor branch to your SOC. This helps the local vendors understand the scope of the mission for your SOC from a company perspective. The paragraph could go something like this:

The [company] SOC is a [name of certification] certified proprietary alarm and video monitoring station located at the [company] headquarters in [state] and is dedicated to serving all [company] personnel and locations. The SOC's mission is to provide [company] with a base of operations for the communication of information and coordination of events affecting [company] facilities and personnel. The [company] SOC is responsible for ensuring the proper installation and receipt of alarm monitoring signals to conduct timely assessment of alarms and dispatching the appropriate personnel accordingly.

ACCOUNT MANAGEMENT

This section is simple to complete. It would list every person affiliated with the national account from the vendor and the client—your company. The list should include at a minimum from the vendor the names and contact information of the national account manager, project manager, invoice or accounts payable manager, and the executive who your national account manager reports to because you will, on occasion, need to go up the chain with issues.

From your company the list should include first and foremost your SOC for any questions at all. But you should also list the names and contact information of your financing department, the member of supply chain responsible for the MSA, the primary corporate security department contact, the SOC manager and/or supervisor. This information helps to inform the local branches and their technicians of whom to call if they have questions regarding any installation questions, service work questions, or billing issues.

INSTALLATION OR SERVICE WORK RESPONSIBILITIES FOR THE VENDOR

Most of the following listed items should be in your MSA contract to ensure that the vendor is obligated to provide:

1. All employees and subcontractors must be US citizens (if necessary).
2. All employees or subcontractors must have background checks completed.
3. All proposals will be processed through the national account manager.
4. Vendor branch project manager must coordinate scheduling work with local site contact and SOC.
5. Use only parts listed in the MSA. Part substitution must be preapproved by appropriate site contact or corporate security contact listed in account management.
6. Vendor is responsible for any applicable fees associated with obtaining permits or necessary certifications.
7. Vendor will leave a copy of any applicable permits with site contact on the first day of work.
8. The appropriate paperwork regarding computer programming will be filled out and submitted to the SOC a minimum of 24 hours prior to the start of installation work.
9. The MAC address of any IDS equipment or video recording device will be provided to the SOC and IT department prior to installation.
10. Vendor will provide connections of all low voltage power supplies to the installed equipment unless told otherwise by the site management.
11. Vendor technicians will always check in with local site designee and the SOC when arriving at the job site.
12. Vendor technicians will call the SOC and test every signal and individual piece of equipment that was newly installed before leaving the premises.

13. Vendor technicians will call the SOC to verify with the SOC that a service request has been completed properly because the SOC can ensure that the device is working properly.
14. Vendor technicians will always check out with local site contact and the SOC before departing the job site at the end of the day.
15. Vendor technician will coordinate with any onsite general contractor or designated site contact for final walkthrough and approval of installation.
16. All keys associated with security equipment will be given to the local site contact.
17. Vendor will provide originals or copies of any documentation consisting of user manuals, programming info, or as-built drawings of the system at no additional charge within 30 days of completion of installation.

YOUR COMPANY RESPONSIBILITIES

Vendors do not do all the work without a teamwork from your company. The following list is an example of what your company's responsibilities would most likely include and should be documented on the requirements form. If your company fails to ensure that these items are met can stall or delay a new installation. Your company responsibilities could include:

1. Providing initial drawings or as-builts of the job site.
2. Provide master building permit number prior to install if required.
3. Provide a list of network connections or phone lines such as:
   a. Network control panel or data server locations.
   b. All IP addresses, subnet masks, default gateways, and phone numbers prior to installation.
   c. List of all IP port numbers for vendor technicians to use for installation.
4. Provide vendor with a schedule for prewire dates, trim-out dates, and complete construction schedule if applicable.
5. Identify for vendor the necessary wall space for installation of control panels.
6. Provide vendor with 110-volt power with locations and amount if necessary.
7. Provide technicians with list of local site contact names, phone numbers, and email addresses along with who will be responsible for signing the certificate of completion after the final walk through and testing of systems.
8. Provide technicians with SOC contact information.
9. SOC will be responsible for programming all PACS, IDS, and VMS equipment.
10. SOC will provide final approval that the install is complete.

SECURITY SYSTEM DESCRIPTIONS

Under this section, you should describe the various systems that your company deploys across your corporation. This should include the standard equipment that your company primarily uses and/or prefers. This should include any special instructions that your company requires such as system design or wiring and programming responsibilities. Be sure to cover the following:

1. PACS—Software, panel types, reader types, motions, and so on.
2. IDS—Software is different from the PACS, panel type, keyboard type, request-to-exit motion (REX), and so on.
3. VMS—Software, preferred recording method such as at the edge or centralized, preferred video recorder, preferred video camera brand types, and so on.

The SOC should be aware of the installation expectations to ensure that you are getting what you paid for at the time of installation. Your SOC will know if you are getting the newer model panel versus an older model, which you may not have paid for.

CHANGE ORDERS

To protect your company from a vendor that likes to add change orders to a new installation after the job survey make sure your contract states that the vendor is responsible for equipment that is necessary to complete the installation that they failed to address during their job survey. However, you might want to make a change during an installation that will require a request for change and a quote. The SOC needs to be made aware of any change orders so they can ensure that the proper item is being installed.

PROJECT COMPLETION OR SITE COMMISSION

The most important part of this section is that the vendor must ensure that all equipment properly reports back to and works as expected with your SOC. This requires that the vendor test every device one at a time to ensure that the proper alarm or video signals are being received correctly in the SOC from the site.

A device list should be prepared by the vendor. For each device, the name as programmed in the system should match the item on the list. Items such as card readers and door contacts should be labeled in accordance with the site users and their onsite language. The vendor technician should have a local site contact with them. As they test each device it should be determined if the door name is correct. If a technician calls a door the rear door but the local site contact calls the door the "back door" as do other people working at the location, then the name that should be programmed into the system should be "back door." That way when someone from the location calls to complain about the "back door" card reader, the SOC staff know exactly which door to look at for status. Correct access control is when an access card with the proper programming is able to grant access to a card reader door and your system should show a "granted access" on your system screen in the SOC. If the door is opened without an access card the system status should show a "door forced" alarm in the SOC. If the door is held open for a specific time such as 2−5 minutes, then the door should show a "door held open" alarm status in the SOC. To some of you reading this that will sound all too common and you're thinking "no duh!" But vendors do not always test such things and will leave the site as quickly as they can if that is not verified. All of that needs to be tested for each device.

IDS devices all need to be tested to ensure accuracy in the SOC. If the vendor technician sets off a motion alarm and the SOC sees it as a glass break alarm, then you know you need to correct the programming. Local onsite users need to be able to arm and disarm the site through the newly installed keypad and the SOC needs to see those actions in their system.

Cameras need to be checked for focus accuracy and motion capabilities if applicable. Vendors should not be allowed to leave a site if a camera is blurry or the default position is pointed backward at a wall. The service technician will need to be on a cell phone with the SOC while they talk them through many of these issues.

Any discrepancies or issues that cannot be fixed quickly on the spot, which need to be scheduled for a later day, should result in a delay of you or another company representative signing off on the certificate of completion (COC). Do not let a vendor tell you that they will fix it tomorrow but need you to sign the COC today. We will admit that we have done that. We have been burned by vendors that claimed they needed the COC signed and then promised to get the job done but do not followthrough or when they do complete the work, the result is a very lazy and/or incompetent job. But the vendor will not take the heat from the site or management, you will. Protect yourself and make your vendors complete the work.

SERVICE CALLS AND WORK ORDERS

Your SOC should be responsible for creating and tracking all service requests to your vendors, to document all systems issues to track completion of service requests and for future reference tracking. This helps if you have a door that is constantly having a problem and you can show that multiple techs have not been able to correct the issue due to inexperience or other reasons. Multiple calls for the same issue should be addressed with your vendor management. Most incident reporting systems can be modified to create tasks that can act as work order ticket tracking for your sites and keeps the information in your IR database that can also be searched for past issues.

Before creating any new work order with a vendor due to system issues, your staff should have attempted all basic actions necessary with your SOC's troubleshooting checklist to correct the problem from your end. If your staff that fails to perform the troubleshooting actions before they dispatch a tech this could result in unnecessary expense for your company. Your staff should state in the work order the following information:

- What site the problem is at?
- Who reported the problem?
- Who the site contact is?
- What troubleshooting attempts were made prior to creating the work order service request?
- What the response and result was with the troubleshooting?
- What the diagnosis may be?

Over time your more experienced SCOs will be able to determine what is a faulty strike and what is a bad card reader.

When placing a work order service request into the vendor, it is important to give them a rating level for the work order so they can prioritize their schedule. In your requirements document, you should create a rating system of how to rate the importance of service calls to the vendor and the timeliness of their repair. That priority number must come from the site designate, the SOC manager or supervisor, or another designee. After the SCO receives the priority, put that number into the work order. Your SCOs should document who they spoke with at the vendor call center. During the call your SCOs should state clearly to the vendor, "This is a number # priority" and the vendor should handle it that way. Some vendors now offer an electronic ticket creation system. It is okay to use those too but our recommendation is that you always follow up a ticket creation by sending the confirmation email to your national or local account manager and project manager for their records.

The following is an example of a work order priority rating system:

Priority Levels

1. ASAP or emergency. Work order should be done the same day if possible. If the work order cannot be done the same day, then the very

next day it should be completed. Call the SOC on call for permission to send a vendor afterhours.

2. Should be completed within 1 business day.
3. Should be completed within 2−3 business days.
4. Can be completed at the earliest convenience.
5. Specific date and/or time needed to complete. For example, any work regarding a specific floor like the executive area should be scheduled soon with a specific date and time. This should be coordinated through dayshift personnel so that they can work with the executive assistants to coordinate the best time possible.

Please keep in mind that this may not actually be the time frame for getting things done. Especially when the vendor may need to order certain parts. It is the SOC's responsibility to ensure that the work orders stay current and that we follow up with the vendor. Anytime you send a follow-up email or make a follow-up call, you must document that action in the follow-up comments of the work order. For example:

> Called vendor for status of parts on order. Spoke to Geoffrey who stated they should be receiving the part next week.

HISTORICAL LESSONS

At one company, we were having major issues with several sites in another state that was installed by a different company from our primary vendor due to budgetary time constraints. The SOC was inundated with false alarms, programming wasn't being done correctly in the SOC because nothing made sense at the sites, and employees were constantly angry due to their access cards not working. The decision was made by McCoy to send Jarpey along with one highly trained and experienced technician from our primary vendor to the state experiencing all the issues and visit each site. The purpose was to test every piece of equipment at each of those sites and fix everything on the spot or create work orders to correct the issue. We would start in the late afternoon, meet with the site security POC to discuss the issues they were experiencing, and then conduct our own tests afterhours, so as not to intrude upon employees during regular working hours. The technician had an interesting time getting all his tools through Transportation Security Administration (TSA) at the airport. What Jarpey and the seasoned technician found was that some things were not wired properly and most everything else was not programmed properly. To fix such things, hardware items and programming issues during the daytime hours would have been impossible because we were consistently making changes and doing panel downloads that affected other readers and devices causing all kinds of problems for employees. By taking the time afterhours, we could work unrestricted without worrying about upsetting employees, make the necessary corrections to get things quickly corrected, and leave the site functioning properly for the first time since the initial installation by the different vendor.

We usually started around 1–2pm and the work would often last until midnight. We did this for a couple of weeks. During the first day of the first week of this project, we received a visit from an employee of the third-party vendor because they somehow had learned what we were doing. We later found out that an employee onsite was a relative of an employee at the vendors. This other vendor assured us that their work was solid that any issues must be related to programming taken place after the SOC took control and was willing to have one of their techs work alongside us to which we agreed. The third-party tech caught up with us around 5pm and bragged about how they were confident that the site we were at was golden because he did it himself. By 8pm the look of embarrassment on his face due to all the mistakes we were finding was quite noticeable and he kept asking how late we were going. When we stated we were staying until completed he'd say "okay me too." By 9pm that other tech had had enough and left for the night. We thought he would join us the next day but for the rest of the project we never saw him again.

CHAPTER 13

Incident Reporting

INTRODUCTION

The documenting of incidents that affect any employee or work location of your company is an essential part of your security department. Your SOC should have the vital role of capturing all IR documentation or phone calls in a centralized incident reporting database that can be utilized by the entire security organization to research past issues, continue documenting further incidents, and conduct analysis. This chapter is not going to tell you the proper ways to write an IR. There are many other books and training materials out there dedicated solely to the purpose of proper IR writing that teach the critical information collection of the who, what, when, where, why, and how of an incident. We recommend that you invest in a couple of them and utilize that training information to properly develop your SOC staff skills. This chapter will provide guidance on how your SOC can be the primary call center for reporting of incidents and collection station for all incidents that have taken place that affect your company.

CONFIDENTIALITY

One of the biggest barriers against having a SOC collect all the IRs is trust. Since an IR could involve confidential and sensitive information, there will be members of upper management, local site management, other departments such as HR, legal, or other entities that truly believe your staff will tell the whole world breaking that confidentiality. You must earn that trust and over time you will if your staff understands the rule. Your staff must understand that providing information to anyone about an incident or investigation about a person to anyone outside the security department or anyone without a need to know is a terminable offense. Period. No second chances. One and done. No exceptions, even if the person is your most valuable and talented SCO. That action sends a clear message if they leak or tell information to someone without proper authorization or clearance, then they know they will be fired immediately upon being caught and there is evidence to

Security Operations Center Guidebook. DOI: http://dx.doi.org/10.1016/B978-0-12-803657-0.00013-1

corroborate their guilt. This directive must be written into your post orders and/or procedures and signed off on by each member of your staff so that each SCO fully understands the ramifications of their actions if they divulge information to anyone without proper authorization or clearance.

YOU MUST HAVE AN ELECTRONIC INCIDENT REPORT FORM

This is nonnegotiable. If you have or are building a SOC then that means your company is large enough to warrant the need then you must act the part and show some technical proficiency and professionalism. You must have an electronic IR form for your SCOs, security officers, and employees to use to create an IR. IRs should no longer be written by hand on paper because handwriting is no longer a required skill and most people nowa-days have poor handwriting qualities. They are a waste of valuable time. If a security officer is handwriting a report then makes a mistake toward the end, then they must start over unless you allow white out or scratching out words that we believe looks unprofessional. Electronic documents written in a word document that can be easily created on a computer allow for spell checks and provide grammar checking tools to ensure a better quality of report with proper spelling and zero or limited grammatical errors that can be presented confidently to your legal or HR without risk of embarrassment. Get rid of the paper.

YOU NEED A CENTRALIZED DATABASE

It goes without saying to any security professional that IRs are important because they provide a documented record of events that have taken place for posterity. There are many different forms of incident management soft-ware available on the market that can be used to capture and manage IRs for your company through your SOC over the course of a calendar year. These software products can also be used to perform security or other types of investigations within your company and allow your security, HR, internal audit or ethics departments to document the entire investigation process to include attached files such as emails, documents, pictures, or video. Most investigations start with a report and from that initial report grow into a required full investigation. Another reason for their usefulness is they have all the sections built into allow your SCOs or security officers to easily follow to write the who, what, when, where, why, and how. The SOC can be one of your company's receiving place for those calls or reports and from within the incident management software the IRs can be elevated to cases with their own case management numbers. Besides IR and case management, these IR software tools usually provide some form of analytics and trend reporting that can help you to identify areas of opportunities to improve or strengthen your physical security posture in the hopes of reducing further IRs. Most of these various software packages provide many other tools that could enhance your security department such as dispatch logs.

At one company, we did not have an incident management software for the first few years. We tracked everything on a spreadsheet and archived the IRs in a shared drive folder. The IR recording number would be the calendar year followed by a number in the order of receipt. For example, the first IR of a calendar year submitted to or created by the SOC would be 2017−0001 and the second would be 2017−0002. The problem with that is IRs would sometimes be assigned a number, and archived but forgotten to be added to the spreadsheet log and then the next SCO would use the same IR number then we'd have overlapping IRs and everything out of chronological order. Something upper management usually frowns upon. When our first IR management software was purchased for that company it simplified our lives in the SOC dramatically and removed those potential errors and allowed us to provide a better finished product with our completed reports.

DIFFERENT MODES OF INCIDENT REPORTING

To ensure that your security department allows employees and company locations the maximum opportunity to report security incidents, do not limit yourself to just one form of receiving IRs. The last thing you want is an employee to call and say they have a report they would like to make, then be told by the SCO that they need to fill out a form. That is just going to turn people off and unless they feel very strongly about reporting the incident, there is a strong chance they will skip it altogether and your security department has just lost potential valuable intelligence from that location about an internal matter that may be serious. There are several different ways your SOC could receive an IR and you should try to utilize as many of them as possible. The various ways to receive an incident that require a need to create a new IR could include:

- Direct phone call to your SOC and report is taken over the phone.
- Online IR form posted on your company's intranet site that employees fill out such as an IR form in a word document that is either faxed (surprisingly some people still use it—NOT recommended) or emailed (recommended) to your SOC.
- Security officer stationed at a site submits a completed report.
- SOC staff must write their own IR due to actions initiated on their part.

The Direct Call

It may seem like it is an unnecessary amount of work for a SCO to stay on the phone for about 10−20 minutes taking a verbal report when they could be doing something else of greater importance. But this way of taking a report should be allowed and encouraged. These calls can come from anyone at all to include employees, contractors, or people completely unaffiliated with your company but they have found or witnessed something that is related to your company that they feel strong enough to report to your security department. If your company has its own public operator that receives calls from customers or anyone outside the company, they should be trained to forward any security-related call to your SOC. That should never be discouraged.

When the SOC receives a phone call from an individual wishing to report an incident, suspicious activity, security concern, or other matter to your SOC, the SCO's job is to communicate professionally and thoroughly with the caller to obtain and document the who, what, when, where, why, and how pertaining to the reason for the call or incident. The SCO should immediately begin to document everything stated to the SCO using the form provided in the incident management software. This is where their training and professionalism needs to shine through. The caller could be agitated, distressed, or even under some form of duress when they call and the SCO will need to reassure the caller that they are there to help. As the SCO is going through each section of the IR and filling in the form with the details of the incident, they must be taught to not be afraid to ask questions of the caller for clarity and additional useful information. Since the person calling may be stressed during the time of their call their thoughts could be flying at a rapid pace and their telephonic story-telling may be incoherent if the SCO does not provide some direction with their requests for information and the questions they ask to fill in the details. In addition to being reassuring, the SCOs must act like they are the first-line investigators of an incident. They must ask questions:

- What happened? Has this happened before? Did you see this happen?
- Who was there with you? Were there any other witnesses? Do you suspect any of your coworkers?
- When exactly did this happen? What date and time specifically?
- Where exactly did this happen? Was it on company property? Was it off site?
- Any idea why this happened? Was this an accident?
- Do you know how this happened? Do you think this was intentional?

The amount of questions that could be asked is practically limitless. The more detail your SOC captures at the time of reporting could pay huge dividends to your corporate security, HR, or departments follow investigation if such a thing is required due to the nature of the report. Recording of all calls going in and out can pay dividends here too. The SCO may not remember to write everything down and they could replay the recorded call afterward to review as insurance they have captured all necessary details in the written report. The recorded call will also help the follow-up investigation if one is required.

Teach your SCOs that before they hang up with the caller to review all the information they have just documented to ensure that it is accurate and detailed. Most likely another little detail will pop into the caller's head and they will add more information to the report that could possibly be quite useful if an investigation is required. Another important step after the review for each SCO has been conducted is finish by adding one last question, "is there anything else you would like to add to this report, no matter how small?" You may be surprised at the little but important details that are produced by conducting a review and asking that one last question before completing the call. The last words to the caller should be the SCO thanking the caller for bringing this situation to their attention and taking the time with them to help get the report completed. This kind and professional act will leave the caller with a sense of good will that they have done the right thing. In the future, they will continue to call back to report other security concerns and encourage others to do the same thing when there is a matter that ought to be reported to security.

Online Incident Report Form

Your security department and your SOC should already have a website of their own location through your company's intranet website to allow your employees to be able to find you easier for reporting and help. Not everyone will want to call because some people might prefer to just write their story and then send it to you for follow-up later. Phone reports usually have a direr sense of urgency but an online report may not require such a greater urgency such as someone accidentally damaging a piece of company property such as a gate access card reader that can be easily rectified in time but needs to be reported nonetheless because the SOC will know it is not working.

The online IR form can be achieved through two different formats. One is through a link posted on your website that is connected to your centralized database software and automatically inputs the report into your system as an alert or notification to be reviewed by the SOC. Your staff would then be responsible for opening the notification and converting it into an actual IR that is assigned a record number. The SCO opening the alert or notification conduct the following:

- Review the alert for details. The SOC may need to call or email the person who created the notification for more detail to add to the IR before sending it up the chain-of-command.

- If additional details are not required, then the SCO should send an email back to the reporting employee (if your IR management software does not do it automatically) letting them know the report has been received, has been saved, and will be forwarded to the proper personnel who may or may not need to follow up with them later.
- Review cameras or access logs if applicable and add that information to the IR.
- Save the information and create the IR. Then forward to proper security management personnel.

The other way to receive online reports, is to work with your local IT department to create an online form. This would allow employees to write their report and click submit that would then go to your SOC's group email box. The same actions above still apply. Instruct IT set the form up to have an automatic return notification. That is good for letting people know that the SOC has received the report, that it will be processed and then sent to the proper management personnel. That communication is important so the reporter does not feel like they just wasted their time. Your SOC email follow-up template or auto-generated communication should read something like this:

> Thank you for submitting your report to the Security Operations Center (SOC). The report will be reviewed and saved in our incident report database then forwarded to the proper management personnel for their further review. If you have any questions or concerns about your report, or would like to add additional information please feel free to contact the SOC directly at the number or email listed below. We are available 24/7 and 365 days a year to help you.
>
> Again, thank you for taking the time to make us aware of this situation. Have a good day.
>
> [Company Name] Security Operations Center
> 800—555—5000 Toll Free
> SecurityOperationsCenter@CompanyName.com

Security Officer from Sites

If your company is fortunate enough to have security officers at your organization's various sites, then that security officer should know that besides their local management contacts all IRs of any nature must be reported to the SOC. It is our recommendation that your company provide computers to those guards so they can also write their report electronically versus handwriting. After a security officer has sent in his or her report to the SOC, the SOC should review for accuracy, detailed information, spelling, and grammar, and if there are any issues then send it back to the security officer for correcting.

SCO Writes their Own Report

The primary purpose of alarm monitoring is dispatching a response to an alarm that has been received. That reason along with perhaps witnessing a crime or violation of corporate policy on the VMS or a security officer has become injured or ill and the SOC has had to dispatch EMTs to help the security officer. These are many other reasons the SCO must write their own IR. When they do they must take care to write the report as detailed and thorough as possible while leaving out personal beliefs and/or opinions. Just the facts. Only the facts. Always document the details no matter how large or small. More often than we care to admit SCOs will not write an IR because they are just not sure that incident requires an IR. If it is not in writing, then it did not happen. The rule to live by for your SOC is "when in doubt, write it out." Your staff should know that motto means if they are unsure whether to write an IR, that they should err on the side of caution and document the incident. That expression has been uttered within the security industry for decades and still applies today in all things related to security.

HISTORICAL LESSONS

Reporting a security concern to your SOC should never be discouraged and everyone that does so ought to be treated graciously as well as professionally, then thanked adamantly for reporting their concern. By allowing staff to call the SOC to report their concerns or issues will only create a strong reputation as a security department that is genuine about doing their jobs to the best of their abilities. The alternative does nothing but create sore feelings plus a bad reputation within the company and things might even roll down the chain-of-command the way most security professionals would care to avoid. We know.

At one company, about a month after the horrible attacks on the United States of America on 9/11, 2001, everyone was still on high alert and anxieties were running high. A vice president (VP) was sitting in his corner office of the main office building where the SOC was also located looking out the window. The VP watched as a truck, which looked like the type used in the Oklahoma City attack, pulled up next to the building on a busy street in our downtown location where parking is not allowed and parked his truck. The driver made a call on his mobile phone all the while looking at our building. The driver then got out of his truck and walked toward our building. The VP became nervous when the "middle eastern looking man" (those are the actual words used by the VP when he called) did not return to his truck after a couple of minutes, the VP decided to call the SOC emergency line to report the incident. The VP informed the SCO who answered the call of what he just witnessed and asked that security check out the truck and look for the driver.

The SCO's response, "don't worry about it." The VP was shocked and became adamant that security needs to do something because it could be another terrorist attack in the heart of a major downtown metropolis. The SCO replied with every ounce of his oratory skills by stating confidently "don't worry about it. It's nothing." The VP, now furious, hangs up the phone and immediately proceeds to directly call the director of the corporate security department and begins to voice his disapproval of the SOC and all things security within the company to the director. After that call is over, the director who is now fully embarrassed and angry proceeds to call the security manager who is responsible for the SOC into his office and begins to use many colorful adjectives in his explanation to the manager about how he will investigate and rectify this situation. The manager then calls the SOC supervisor and in a gentler but no less firm tone explains that the SOC supervisor will resolve this situation ASAP and report back to the manager in person with the results. The supervisor then walks into the SOC, looks at the cameras, and sees a truck on the side of the building. The supervisor asks the two SCOs on duty "anybody know why that truck is sitting there on the street and where the driver is?" The SCO who originally answered the VP's call replied, "Yes I found he is in the loading dock waiting to pull down because they are full right now." The supervisor looked at the loading dock cameras and verified the SCO's statement then asked, "Did either of you get a call from a VP asking about that guy's truck and his concern over the driver?" The SCO who took the call answered happily and quite pleased with himself, "Yes I told him it was nothing to worry about." <Sigh>.

To make a longer story shorter, the end result was that the supervisor was on the receiving end of a lengthy verbal counseling session by both the manager and director on the importance of quality customer service, professionalism by security and SOC staff when dealing with our internal customers, and taking security reports or concerns of the utmost seriousness. The SCO received a written counseling session on the very same topics in addition that the supervisor received in a very similar manner along with using being courteous, professional, and how to use proper phone etiquette. This large amount of drama in one day could have easily been avoided if the SCO said the following statement to the VP, "We saw that too. What we found was that driver is waiting to pull down into our dock because its full. The driver is in our dock now talking to our shipping & receiving manager. Thank you, sir, for reporting this to us though. We appreciate you staying alert." That would have ended the call right there and the VP would have been happy knowing he did the right thing and that he has a quality security department that is alert and looking out for his fellow employees and the company. Proper phone etiquette with a courteous manner along with quality communication is important to building a strong reputation as a professional SOC that wants to receive those IRs.

CHAPTER 14

Communication Plan

INTRODUCTION

As stated earlier, the primary goal of the SOC is to observe and report, then communicate and coordinate. Communication is essential to the success of your SOC. If your applicants do not have good speaking or writing capabilities, then they should not be hired. Your SCO's primary responsibility is communicating about events and updating those that are in positions of responsibility by sending notifications to ensure that they are aware of the status of the incident. Remember, SCOs should not be placed in a position that they are making decisions about what to, they should be following their post orders that instruct them to take steps such as dispatching security officers, law enforcement, fire department, and/or emergency medical technicians. There are several different forms of communication your SCOs will be using in your SOC to include telephones, cell or mobile phones, handheld radios, pagers, fax machines, email, intercoms, overhead building paging system, perhaps different forms of instant messaging software, and a mass notification alert system. One thing we do not recommend is video communications because that is a distraction from other duties such as alarm monitoring and writing reports. We know some company's love to have video webcams at everyone's desk for face-to-face communication but in the case of the SOC all you are doing is taking your SCO's eyes off their VMS or IDS monitors so they can look at a webcam. Does not make sense. Another reason for not adding webcams into your SOC is the sensitive nature of what you do at times, your SOC might have a posting of a terminated employee hanging on a poster board and that might be visible in the background. You cannot have customers video conferencing into your SOC and run the risk of them seeing something confidential that they should not. The following will help you plan for how your SOC will communicate to your company.

COMMUNICATING CORPORATEWIDE

Never stop until contact is made. Depending on the level of incident that is being reported should be the motto behind your SOC's communication

Security Operations Center Guidebook. DOI: http://dx.doi.org/10.1016/B978-0-12-803657-0.00014-3

plan. Why? Because once your staff has notified the appropriate personnel, they have accomplished their primary mission. There will most likely need to be continued updates but now the proper management personnel have been mobilized and/or engaged. They should be able to provide additional guidance and/or leadership on continuing actions. Not everything needs to be hound dogged until someone has been notified by phone. For example, if an employee accidentally sets off a building alarm at zero dark forty in the morning the first thought by a SCO should not be "I've got to call security management!" Their site procedures should be written where their priority is investigating the alarm to determine the actual cause of the alarm. If they contact the employee and verify they are the person is an actual employee resulting in the fact that the alarm was false, the SOC still has to notify someone but it does not have to be by telephone. An email along with and IR sent to the site responsible person(s) is enough to let that site management know that something happened, the SOC acted and discovered all was well. Why do this? Two reasons, reputation and word gets around. Your SOC will gain the reputation as being alert and vigilant, thus building the confidence of management that your staff is taking care of your locations by doing their jobs to the utmost of their ability. Word will get around the site if the manager contacted talks to the employee saying, "I got an email from the SOC saying you accidentally set off the alarm." Other employees will see that employee talking to the manager and ask what their conversation was about. When the employee informs them of the SOC's notification of his or her mistake when setting off the building alarm upon entry, other employees now know that the alarm did not go undetected and the SOC acted quickly. A better example of this if the SOC witnesses something that they know is against company policy and they report it, which ends with disciplinary action against the employee(s), people will understand that it came from the SOC. Some employees hate these cameras and the company's card access tracking and complain about it being big brother watching but we as security professionals know that cameras and card access are a strong deterrent to activity that is against company policy.

There are incidents that need to be reported immediately and these should be written as such in your post orders or site procedures. These include but are not limited to the following:

- Dispatching any form of emergency services such as police, fire, or medical response.
- Any form of emergency services just show up at a location.
- Loss of life on company property.
- Bodily injury on company property.
- Firearms usage on company property.
- Theft of company or employee property.

- Trespassing on company property.
- Any criminal activity.
- Damage to company property.
- Environmentally hazardous incident such as chemical or oil spill.
- Major incidents to include fire, explosions, any other event such as the previous listed ones or any incident that could result in media attention to the company and/or that specific location.

Those types of incidents require the SOC to act such as dispatching emergency response forces or acquire as much of the who, what, when, where, why, and how of the incident and notify the proper personnel what has taken place.

NOTIFICATION LISTS ALSO KNOWN AS CALL TREES

Your emergency procedures for every major incident should have a minimum of at least three people listed on whom to contact for notification in the event of a company emergency. These can be broken down by site, or business unit as decided by management. Corporate security should always have an afterhours call list for any major event affecting a site. That list should contain the following:

1. The SOC supervisor
2. The SOC manager
3. The on-call duty officer for corporate security (if applicable)
4. The director of corporate security
5. The chief security officer

The SOC should have each individuals work, cell, home, and pager numbers (if still being used) plus any other number that each person may spend a large amount of time at such as a vacation home. Your SOC staff should know that they always have someone to call with questions or in the event of an emergency.

For most situations, they will involve a particular site and your SOC may have to notify people who are affiliated with that site of the incident and/or emergency response personnel. Your site procedures should have all the applicable contact personnel in the site procedure for that location. The following is the minimum they should have on hand but is not limited to:

1. The primary, secondary, and third POC for the site. More if necessary, depending on site priorities. For example, one area of a building may have completely different contacts than the rest of the location. For SCO convenience, break the information down into regular business hours and afterhours order.

2. Emergency services—both emergency and nonemergency contact numbers. If your sites being monitored are out of your local town or city jurisdiction, such as another state or county, then the SOC is not going to be able to call 911 from their phones, they will need to call the site's local dispatch numbers for emergency services and it will take some research. It is best to be prepared in advance, so your staff is not wasting time searching online for a number or calling local 911 and asking them to transfer, because they will not like that. Ensure that you have the numbers in your site procedures for the following because they may not always be the same:
   a. Site local police department.
   b. Site local fire department.
   c. Site local sheriff.
   d. Site local emergency medical technician or paramedics.
3. The local power company. If power goes down for that site, your SOC should have the phone number of the power company to notify in case the facility manager is not available to make the power company aware of the outage.
4. The local phone or Internet provider company. Your IT department usually has that information but it does not hurt to also have it on hand.

Your SCOs must work together and shout out to each what actions they are taking so the other knows who is doing what. Your SOC might even receive other calls during this moment and if the call does not pertain to the current emergency, the SOC may have to tell the caller that they will need to call them back due to handling an emergency. We will use an example of a fire taking place at a building after the site has closed for the day.

1. SOC receives fire alarm.
2. First SCO who acknowledges the alarm makes second SCO on duty aware of the situation: "We've got a fire alarm at the warehouse!" Then quickly begins to call local fire department (FD) for immediate response.
3. Each action taken by one SCO should be immediate relayed to the other SCO, so they are not repeating actions that have already been taken.
4. Second SCO pulls up all cameras located onsite at the warehouse and begins to review for fire, then checks access to see if anyone has used their access card on site since building closure. Second SCO sees smoke in a hallway camera that is facing an entrance door but no current card activity then reports his or her findings to the first SCO who should relay that information to the FD dispatcher.
5. Second SCO opens the site procedures for the location and begins to call the primary contact for the location. Second SCO tries the cell

and then the home number of the primary contact with no answer and leaves messages on both lines.

6. Second SCO then attempts to call secondary contact and the home phone is answered. Second SCO reports to secondary contact that the SOC has received a fire alarm, they can see smoke on one hallway camera but there is no current card activity. Secondary contact states that they will report to the site.

7. First SCO continues to monitor for FD arrival and places all card readers in unlock mode to ensure that they have immediate access (yes, most fire alarms will automatically unlock the doors but it never hurts to be sure).

8. First SCO observes that FD arrives onsite and lets shift partner know. FD enters the location to find that a defective space heater was the cause of the smoke.

9. Second SCO observes that local police department (PD) arrives onsite and lets shift partner know.

10. Second SCO notices that site secondary contact arrives onsite and lets shift partner know. The contact is seen on the exterior camera reporting to the FD captain and PD.

11. FD inspects entire site for other potential fire hazards and upon finding no other present danger issues an "all clear" and then departs the site. PD follows FD offsite. Both SCOs are observant and have written down the responding vehicle numbers of both FD and PD.

12. First SCO calls the contact located on premises and receives their statement of what has just taken place and their actions. This includes the name of the employee who left the defective space heater on.

13. First SCO begins to write the incident report while the second SCO begins to archive all the video from the event for posterity. Important items to capture in IR:
    a. Time of receipt of alarm.
    b. Time of dispatch.
    c. Time of calls to contacts.
    d. Time of FD, PD, and site contact arrival.
    e. All actions taken by the SCOs, FD, PD, and site contact.

14. First SCO notifies corporate security management and provides a recap of the incident. If security management requests any other actions as follow up to the incident, the SCOs would document that in the IR.

15. Second SCO calls primary contact and leaves messages letting them know that the situation was resolved.

16. First SCO completes writing of IR and second SCO reviews for accuracy of timing and details.

17. First SCO saves IR and sends a copy of it to the site management and corporate security management.
18. End of incident and notifications.

No two scenarios are alike, which means your SOC staff must be prepared for various situations that may arise. Some notifications may not need a phone call. If your SOC receives an "At Wrong Door" alarm because someone attempted access into an area they are not authorized, your SOC should be sending an email to the site's proper management personnel letting them know that an unauthorized person attempted access. The majority of the time it is nothing nefarious but most likely a person is just curious if they have access into that area. However, by making a restricted area manager or site security manager of such an attempt builds trust with those people that your SOC is doing their job. If your SOC receives an alarm due to a lost card that is being used to try and gain access to a site, they should verify that it was not an attempt by someone who found the card on the street either through video review or by calling the owner of the card to verify the attempted usage. Most likely the employee found the lost card and is wondering if it stills works. Your SOC should send an email to those responsible for that area letting them know that an attempt was made by that employee to use a card that was previously reported lost. Below are examples of the email that can be sent from your SOC to make your customer aware of what has happened at their site.

Example Emails to Send from the SOC

When responding to a customer via email in regard to a lost card, card expired, or at wrong door/time alarm, follow the examples below.

Lost Card Usage Example

CC the person's supervisor also.

[Card holder name and site responsible person]

The card that you reported lost [number], was used to attempt access at [location] on [date] at [time]. If you have found this card, please return it to the SOC by mailing it to the address shown on the back of the card.

If you have not found this card and believe that someone else could have it in his or her possession, please let the SOC know ASAP.

Please contact the SOC with any information that may help resolve this issue.

You may reach the SOC at 555–555–5001. You may also send an email explanation or inquiry to the SOC at: Soc@company.com

Thank you for your assistance and have a good day!

[SCO Signature Block]

Card Expired Example

[Supervisor name], You are listed as the supervisor for [Card holder name]. [Card holder name], badge [number], came up card expired at [location] in our system on [date] at [time]. The card shows that it has been de-activated [reason (found in notes section)]. Please contact the SOC with any information that may help resolve this issue.

You may reach the SOC at 555–555–5001. You may also send an email explanation or inquiry to the SOC at: Soc@company.com

Thank you for your assistance and have a good day!

[SCO Signature Block]

MASS NOTIFICATION ALERT SYSTEM

Internet-based mass notifications systems are becoming more popular with corporations, hospitals, schools, and government entities, and are used as a form of communication during a crisis or other event that may affect a location. It is up to your company to define what a crisis is or what the mass notification system will be used for. There are several different examples that the notification system could be used for such as the list of items noted earlier in this chapter that need to be reported immediately and the action prescribed by management. These examples include but are not limited to the following:

1. Fire on premises, evacuate immediately.
2. Hazardous chemical spill, evacuate immediately.
3. Active Shooter or Active Hostile on premises or in building. Take appropriate action.
4. Site power outage. Do not report to work.
5. Severe weather—due to heavy snowfall all employees are instructed to work from home or take a PTO day.
6. This list is only limited by your creativity and how you use your mass notification system.

There are other departments that may believe they should manage the alert system such as risk, safety, or IT, and perhaps they have access to the system to send out the alerts but your SOC should be the primary administrators of the system. The reasons for this are simple, risk and safety are not going to have people on duty during the middle of the night. IT may have their own SOC or call center on duty 24/7, but they are more focused on network security and server rooms. Your SOC's primary concern is the safety and security for all personnel and property of your company. Some of the alert system duties could easily be split with IT and that is okay because both entities may need to use the system for different reasons but your staff should have full admin rights to be able to create alert templates, modify alerts, updating personnel information when new information has been presented to the SOC.

MASS NOTIFICATION ALERT AUTHORIZATION LISTS

There should be an alert authorization list at the corporate level, the business unit, or subsidiary level and each site should have a list of who is authorized to send out an alert to that site. Most lists will include various managers from operations, facilities, safety, HR, and always security. The site level lists should be saved with your site procedures for easy recall. There should also be a written contingency in your post orders or site procedures that if an unauthorized person from a site calls requesting a site wide alert that the SOC contact the SOC supervisor, SOC manager, or corporate security management immediately for authorization. The SOC should never turn any employee away from requesting an alert because the situation could be one that requires an alert and those on the authorized lists may not be available.

Each authorization list should also document the various applicable distribution lists that may need to be created for an alert and the names of those authorized to send out an alert to that distribution list (DL). An example of the various DLs created in your mass notification system could include but are not limited to:

1. All personnel assigned to the site.
2. All management personnel only.
3. All security personnel only.
4. All safety personnel only.

SOC'S POSITIVE RESPONSE TO AN ALERT REQUEST EQUALS REGULAR TRAINING

The SOC being contacted to create an alert for an actual event or crisis may be nerve wracking for your SCOs because if it is real situation versus a drill they know they must get it right the first time because there is no recall on alerts. Once the alerts are sent they are not coming back. If they go out wrong your whole SOC staff takes a black eye in the reputation department. You must train and practice with your SCOs on creating these alerts because they will find themselves getting anxious or nervous due to the fact that they know this is a serious matter. You must train them to remain calm, take a deep breath, and remember to be meticulously thorough by collecting all the proper information, and not rush frantically to get the alert created and sent. To avoid the overrushed nervousness that comes with creating an alert you have to conduct practice drills. Coordinate with personnel at each site and arrange times for key management personnel, then call your SOC to request that an alert be sent for various plausible reasons, and have the caller act as if the situation is real. This will provide real-world training to your SCOs so they get the feel of sending out an alert under stressful terms. The more your SCOs practice this the more confident they will become and be able to handle a real-world situation that may be truly stressful if the alert is related to a life-threatening incident.

Alert Request Sample Procedure

Your staff needs to have an idea of how these calls will happen and what they should do when they receive a request for an alert being put out. The call usually starts with someone calling the SOC under some minor or major form of stress due to an incident that has taken or is taking place currently onsite with the statement, "I need to have an alert sent out." The following is a list of steps that could be utilized for your SCOs to use when receiving such a call. The order may need to change per your company's policies but this is an example:

1. Ask the caller's name and what site they are calling from. If the SOC does not personally know the employee, they will need to ask some questions to verify ID.
2. Inform the caller you need to verify their identity to ensure they are an actual employee.
3. Verify their employee ID or badge number then check to ensure they have an active access card in your ACS.
4. Check the employee online directory and using the information in either the ACS or employee directory, inform the employee that you need to ask them a couple of questions such as:
5. If they answer 1–3 answers correctly and you are positive the caller is who they say they are you can begin to work with them on sending out the alert.
6. Assure the caller you will help them get the alert. Ask them to be patient with you while you assist them and ask what type of alert and who exactly they want it to go out to.
7. Verify they are authorized to have an alert sent out.
8. Select the correct template or create a new one if necessary. If using a template, read the customer exactly what the template says and if there is anything they want to add or amend.
9. Select the requested DLs and ask if there is anyone else they want to add or if they approve of the final selection.
10. Once the caller fully approves of the alert type, the verbiage of the alert and the DLs selected, you should then select the alert.

Depending on exactly what type of situation is happening at that site, all the above could go out the window. If some person called the SOC to report an active shooter at XYZ site and the SOC pulls up the site's cameras in the VMS only to find people running and laying on the ground, then action ought to be to one SCO calls 911 for that location while the other sends out the alert.

Threat Management Teams

There are several different resources available for the practice of workplace violence assessment, intervention, and response, and we recommend that you read several books and attend classes on the topic of workplace violence. Threat management teams are responsible for evaluating and developing a plan of action related to all threats of violence, aggression, threats, or unethical, or unbecoming conduct involving employees. If your site uses this system of threat management team (TMT), then it is highly recommended that your SOC be used to send out an alert as needed to convene a TMT to meet or call into a conference call to discuss a situation. There should be a master list of TMTs and each person on that list is authorized to request that an alert be sent for the location(s) they are listed under.

Crisis Management Teams

Some companies utilize a crisis management team (CMT) for each site, business unit, or subsidiary and corporate level staff to mobilize or respond to an event affecting one of those sections. Often the CMT personnel will be wearing dual hats and be the same as the TMT personnel with one or two exceptions. The SOC should have the list of each CMT and everyone on that list is authorized to call the SOC to request an alert, same as the TMTs. One thing you will need to determine is whether or not you want the SOC included on any conference call to see if there is any support they could provide each company is different on how they prefer to handle that.

HISTORICAL LESSONS

Knowing that the SOC is watching and acting on alarms they receive or things they witness on the VMS, then communicating that information to the proper personnel is what you want your company to believe. At one company, we had an employee pull his car up to the shipping and receiving dock on a Saturday afternoon when the site is normally closed and begin to load up three large boxes into the back of his vehicle. The SCO on duty knew this was not a normal activity, so they reported it to the SOC management who instructed the SCO to put together an access report along with video and a suspicious activity report and send it to them and copy the security on-call duty officer for Monday follow up. The security investigator on Monday talked to the manager of the location who had no idea what the employee might be doing and was worried that this might be a form of theft asked security to handle the situation. The security investigator joined the manager at the site to jointly talk to the employee. This site was small enough to know that someone from corporate security was onsite and in some companies, that makes people nervous. When the manager asked the employee to join him and the security in the manager's office you can imagine how many neighboring employee's eyes got wide very quickly. The story has a happy ending when it was discovered that a different employee who was working as a representative of the company at community event realized that they forgot the company information materials and swag giveaways asked the employee to pick up the boxes and bring it to him at the event. This was all verified by the other employee who was embarrassed that his forgetfulness caused "such a ruckus." Afterward, that site never had anyone enter or leave without contacting the SOC to let them know what they were doing.

At one company, we had an explosion happen in one building at a multi-building campus. Thankfully, there was no loss of life but there were injuries. A member of the crisis team immediately called the SOC frantic and requesting an alert with a conference call be set up. Fortunately, two of our more experienced SCOs were on duty, knew who the caller was, and sprung quickly into action. One SCO sent out the alert with conference call information attached and the other notified corporate security. Members of the corporate security team immediately reported to the SOC and joined the conference call in there. During the call, security questions were asked such as "do we have enough security staff onsite?' among others that the corporate security staff could look to the SCOs on duty for quick answers and they could provide that information quickly to those on the CMT call, which included the CEO. The request for extra security personnel to be brought on duty to help coordinate with emergency response personnel was made by the executive staff and the SOC quickly relayed that information to the contract security provider who assured corporate security management that they would meet the request as fast as possible which they did. The conference call lasted over 2 hours while actions were coordinated and planned during the call until the situation had been contained. The SOC later received recognition from the executive staff for their quick performance and actions. The key to this success was getting the alert out quickly with the conference call information to bring all the appropriate crisis management personnel together to work through the situation. Having two well-trained SCOs on duty were the primary factors in turning that key.

CHAPTER 15

The Emergency Operations Center

INTRODUCTION

Most of this book is about what a SOC can do to support your company during normal daily operations. But what happens when there is a true emergency or crisis event that interrupts normal business operations? Just what that event is, can vary greatly depending on the type of business you support, but the first example is when a security incident occurs and the scope of the event exceeds what can be called normal business. We realize this is a bit vague, but that incident event threshold can change over time within the same company based on the opinion of those in charge at the executive level, to the CSO, and the experience level of the SOC staff.

The primary purpose of an emergency operations center (EOC) is the place where your crisis management teams work with those who help or conduct the coordination of response and recovery efforts in response to the emergency and/ or recovery effort. This crisis management effort can be accomplished in the same building or conducted online through teleconferencing or video conferencing or a combination thereof. When building, or developing your SOC, think forward and imagine the "what if?" What if a hurricane slams into your sites impacting supply chain, sales, and displacing hundreds of employees? What if a building is flooded? What if a tornado strikes one of your properties? What if there is a massive fire or explosion? What if there is an active shooter in a building? Will the SOC become the EOC for your company? Our recommendation is YES. But these are questions you and your upper management will need to ask yourself as you move forward with creating or taking your SOC to the next level. Much of what we have learned about being an effective EOC started during the horrible terrorist attacks of September 11, 2001, and like most companies and colleagues in the security industry continued to learn, grow, and evolve.

WHY THE SOC IS A THE PLACE FOR YOUR EOC

Some companies have built full-blown crisis command centers to use as their areas of operation when responding to and managing a disaster that affects

Security Operations Center Guidebook. DOI: http://dx.doi.org/10.1016/B978-0-12-803657-0.00015-5

their company. We have toured some of these and seen staff sitting there monitoring the weather patterns across the globe, the local, national, and global news along with various intelligence notification services, which is something the SOC can easily do too but the command center personnel are otherwise just sitting there waiting for a crisis to happen. It is great that these businesses take emergency management seriously and have taken such steps to build a command center or EOC but are there really that many crises out there that require full-time staff dedicated to emergency management? The answer is NO. Security officers and SCO's that are good at their jobs will learn during their shifts, the daily ins and outs of a company, and their sites along with various patterns of how the people work there during regular business and afterhours' worktimes. If you are reading this and have never worked as a guard post in your life, then believe us when we tell you that a competent security officer will be able to tell you who the usual people are who work late on a regular and consistent basis. We know because both of us have spent time sitting posts in the early days of our security careers. Sites without security officers that SCOs know they are the primary watchman for that site will be able to tell you when key management personnel come and go and what time the place is usually locked down for the night, and when they really need to pay attention to alarms and cameras because the site has closed. By knowing how the company operates, those SCOs and the security officers they interact with daily will be a key resource of information for anyone working a crisis management event. Their understanding of company patterns and personnel activity will make them invaluable during your crisis management event. Therefore, it is essential to have a confident, educated, and highly competent SOC manager who is the true liaison among the upper management, the crisis management personnel, and SCOs and security officers. That is why we recommend a SOC supervisor as well as the manager because if the SOC manager is unavailable such as being on PTO or on business travel, you should always have someone ready to step up to the next level.

Some companies will be the exception such as power companies that have command centers to handle power outages across their services territories. They don't need any assistance from the SOC for operational outage emergencies. But what about all the other things that can go wrong in a company of that size and complexity? That power company command center should not be distracted trying to handle nonoperational events, their job is too critical. This could be something as localized as protestors causing property damage in a city where your headquarters are located, to a natural disaster that is impacting your entire region. The command center needs to focus on coordinating the repair of whatever damage is taking place, but they don't have time to deal with other business interruptions. This is an excellent example of why the SOC should never be called a command center, but an

EOC. The SOC doesn't command anything, but they do oversee security operations and act as a conduit for communication during crises so that operational people can focus on their job. But the command center and the SOC will need to communicate. You must have a communication plan in place. In this instance, and many others where operational groups need to coordinate, the SOC's job is simple if you go back to the mission statement. Communicate and coordinate information that is affecting your company. The SOC and your staff are the owners and initiators of the emergency operations and various communication tools such as mass notification system or other forms of communication. The SOC can set up the conference call through the mass notification system and the command center can call into the meeting. Once there, they can communicate about the event, refer to documentation that is stored there for reference and a log is kept of everything that is said if you are recording your telephone conversations or have assigned someone to keep a running log. Decisions can be made and actions tracked. From there the team can follow a rigorous process already documented or make it up as they go along. They can call back for updates hourly or leave the line open for the duration of the crisis until recovery mode has started. These tools are essential for good communication and coordination during an emergency, and the SOC's main function is to start the process when some threshold has been reached or they are told to by someone on an authorization list. As stated many times before, the SOC should never be put in a position where they are the ones to make decisions, only to carry out instructions or follow documented procedures. The decisions must be made by someone higher up in security or upper management in the case of a companywide emergency. While there has been a move over the last decade toward a virtual command center as described above, there is also a benefit for some organizations to have a physical place to meet. We are not recommending that the SOC fill that role, but if space is available, having such a room within or directly next to the SOC can be beneficial.

NO ONE SIZE FITS ALL

Have a vision in mind when to start to create your SOC/EOC. We know from experience that when a company decides they need a SOC that it usually starts in a small room, which we know from some colleagues in the industry, which is sometimes no larger than a supply closet and security management must request for more room or space to expand operations as the need has presented itself. When building your SOC, if you are one of the fortunate ones who works for a company with focused forward thinking and are given a proper amount of building space, then you should plan on having an area away from the main SOC room for your executive management and/or crisis management personnel to congregate yet stay close to the main area of communication. The reason for this is the last thing you want is a member of the C-suite hovering over one of your SOC staff questioning every move the SCO makes or asking about all the different programs that are running on the SCO's monitors.

This is detrimental for a couple of reasons, one, it will make the SCO nervous to have someone high up the chain-of-command question every little task they perform and two, this will severely distract them from doing their duties that they need to perform. There needs to be some physical separation and hopefully noise reduction so that both groups can work effectively, but the proximity can save time and eliminate miscommunication that can sometimes occur when not face-to-face. The room can be connected to the SOC but should be walled off from the SOC so they can focus on their jobs. This separate room should have plenty of power outlets, telephones, and video monitoring equipment along with video conferencing equipment, and can see into the SOC or have a camera with a monitor that watches the SOC. At one company, we created the EOC area with video monitors and cable news in the corporate security office for management to congregate during a security crisis versus running into the SOC. Making this happen within your company will depend on the vision you have for your SOC/EOC along with the budget and square foot space available.

What is your EOC supposed to do? How your SOC/EOC fits into your corporate crisis management plan depends upon the resources and tools your company has available or is willing to invest into the idea of the SOC/EOC. This chapter is not meant to teach you how to build your EOC, it is meant to convince you that much of what a SOC must do is already in place for an EOC. There are several resources available such as various books and training classes to help you develop your crisis management plans and how an EOC becomes a part of that process.

Your SOC already has emergency response plans for basic things such as fire, severe weather, and other situations written into their post orders along with supporting threat management teams and crisis management teams for events that require an EOC is a natural extension for the SOC to be your EOC, if a real emergency affecting your business requires your company to activate its crisis management plan. We have shown in previous chapters that your SCOs are already being trained to work during events that are real emergencies because of their alarm monitoring, video surveillance monitoring, their incident reporting, and their emergency notifications through call trees and/or mass notification systems.

Our recommendation is that you must practice and drill your crisis management and EOC activation plans to ensure that you work out all the deficiencies. You will be amazed at how much you learn when you practice your plan and discover where you need to create new actions or plans, modify existing written plans, or remove unnecessary steps or plans altogether. You cannot practice or drill just once after you have successfully completed writing your crisis management and EOC activation plans, this must be an ongoing practice. At a minimum of twice a year or more if possible your company should run a drill to test the level of accuracy for your crisis and EOC plans to determine if updating is needed. All companies go through turnover as employees leave the company or move into new managerial positions where they may have greater participation responsibilities in the crisis and EOC plan. This is also important for your SOC staff, which will go through turnover and new SCOs are hired. How will these new company employees and SCOs know what to do if your company does not complete regular practice drills? Failure to practice means that you are gambling with your plan and hoping that it will work. Performing regular recommended drills will ultimately determine how successful your company and your SOC will be during a real emergency.

HISTORICAL LESSONS

"Greg you're going to want to see this," is what one SCO shouted to SOC manager Jarpey after the first plane hit the north tower. Jarpey entered the SOC from his attached office and watched the news looking at the smoke pouring from the north tower. Jarpey could not believe that a plane accidentally hit the tower on such a beautifully sunny day and continued to stare in amazement at the TV. Jarpey watched live as the second plane purposefully hit the south tower. After the shock of witnessing such an event began to settle down we realized that our country was being attacked. Jarpey called McCoy, who was offsite attending a vendor meeting, to inform him of the situation. McCoy could not believe what he was hearing but stated he was on the way in. One of corporate security investigators who was in the office that day called the local Federal Bureau of Investigation (FBI) office to ask what we as a company should do. The FBI asked that we take all precautions and lock everything down until the event has been resolved. After being quickly approved by the upper management, the order was given to Jarpey to have the SOC lock down the entire company that had sites based in several states. The work of locking everything down was divided among the SCOs on duty and they along with Jarpey began to call sites security POCs to inform them of what was happening. Shortly thereafter, the phones in the SOC began to ring like crazy as people began calling the SOC to ask either why everything was locked or wanting to know if have we seen the news and what should they be doing. At this company, we did our best to feed information up the chain-of-command so they could make the best decisions, and on that day, the SOC was flooding with directors and VPs flowing in and out of the SOC to watch the news unfold while standing next to or behind SCOs and wanting to know every little click they made or who they just spoke to on the phone. That SOC was decent-sized, but it was not meant to have a dozen or more extra people loitering around while carrying on conversations when both operators are working on the phones and collecting information from the sites. Some non-SOC personnel even began to cry or express anger as reports of the Pentagon being struck or the news of flight 93 crashing was reported. Fortunately for us, our VP was in the SOC as this began and was as smart as she was tough. Once McCoy pointed out the problem of all the distractions, she ordered everyone to clear the room and convene at a different location. At the time, this company lacked a mass notification tool, so the SOC set up a regular conference call with hourly updates.

A few months after 9/11, we got a confused report of a plane flying into one of our plants in another state. Our first thought was "here we go again." We still did not have a mass notification system and our procedure for switching from normal SOC operations to EOC was in draft form. We physically searched out our VP and informed her of the incident along with our lack of details. We were unable to get anyone at the plant in question to answer a phone, so we resorted to calling others who might know including a security vendor who was working at the location and watched as the small two-person plane flew into the plant smokestack. Eventually, we got the full story. There was a rare thick and heavy fog covering the area around the plant and a small light plane being flown by an elderly couple mistook the emergency warning lights on the plant for the nearby airports runway lights and flew into the smokestack killing the couple and causing significant damage to the plant. It was not a terrorist attack, just a very unfortunate accident that was being handled by the emergency and first responders at that plant along with local police, fire, and Emergency Medical Technicians (EMTs). Every plant has an emergency plan and they all run drills. They have the gear and experience to deal with most situations including fires. The SOC was only a distraction to them as they dealt the emergency, but upper management including the CEO was not getting update from the business. The business was busy but the communication department and HR and other departments in the corporate needed to be informed and in real time. Just like the room full of executives only distracted the workers and hindered their ability to deal with the emergency, so do people on the ground need to focus on fighting a fire and not on updating the corporate. Certainly at least one person on site needs to take on that role, but instead of fielding dozens of calls and sharing the same information dozens of time, the SOC can bring some order to the chaos and allow for the sharing of information in real time.

We both concur that 9/11 has been overused as an example of anything related to crisis or security management or when a SOC goes into emergency mode but that is because it is the worst domestic event that has ever happened in most people's lives. 9/11 followed by the anthrax attacks, and the beltway sniper had everyone on high alert along with feeling great anxiety and everyone kept waiting for the next big attack. We know now that no other major attack happened until many years later when the shootings at Fort Hood took place, but while the effects of 9/11 was unfolding, it seemed highly likely that there would be more attacks in other parts of the country on that day and in the days to follow. The safety of all Americans was in question for the first time in years and a company has a responsibility to try protecting their employees during a crisis or at least show they have a plan and the capability to respond and in both of those cases written here in the lessons, in addition to the plant explosion in the previous chapter. The real-life example stories we provided in this chapter have demonstrated how a SOC can help your organization and those were both before formal plans were written into place. This is a strong statement that makes it clear through these past experiences of ours how your SOC can and should be the EOC for your company.

Making the SOC an Integral Part of Your Company

CHAPTER 16

Customer Service is Key

INTRODUCTION

Traditionally, a corporate security department doesn't spend a lot of time thinking about customer service. Most focus on regulatory compliance, access control, loss prevention, and so on. In the last 15 years, some companies have moved toward centralization and the inevitable outcome of a shared services organization. Security departments may or may not be included in that group, but since the only constant in business anymore is change, it may only be a matter a time before you find yourself in that position. In this chapter, we are going to try and convince you that regardless of where you currently report or how your company is structured, you should care about customer service.

The reason is simple. We have never seen a security department that did not have to justify its existence and fight for resources. Even if you are currently not in that position, you may be months away from having a new CEO or being involved in a merger where the new leadership will ask 'are we getting our money's worth?'

WHAT DOES YOUR COMPANY NEED FROM SECURITY?

You need to start thinking about the employees and business units in your company as customers and every company has to think "what can I do to keep my customer happy?" Odds are you are in the overhead somewhere since it is unlikely that you generate revenue. The kindest thing we've been called over the years was a necessary evil. Still a little harsh, but at least the word necessary was in there. The worst was having out budget referred to as a burden.

Let's also be clear about what we aren't recommending. We are not recommending you to care about how someone feels after you've interviewed them and worked with HR to terminate them. People terminated for cause will not be getting a transactional survey to find out how their experience could be improved. Nor are we suggesting that you should let people violate policy so they like your more.

153

Security Operations Center Guidebook. DOI: http://dx.doi.org/10.1016/B978-0-12-803657-0.00016-7

What we are saying is that your department provides a lot of services to the company. Most are required, but some could be voluntary. Even the simple act of issuing a badge or changing someone's access could either be a nightmare worse than most department of motor vehicles (DMV) experiences, or it could be fast and painless. What most people want, especially when it comes to things they have to do, is for it to be fast and painless. The business would also prefer it not be radically expensive.

A security department is a busy place and is often filled with people that, let's be honest, are not usually seen as ambassadors of good will. Having your SOC be the main interface between the department and the rest of the company is a logical choice, but even then, the tone of the operators in the SOC is controlled by the department. If they are allowed to be rude or abrupt, most people's experiences will be negative. When something is made unpleasant, it is often circumvented. This is counter to good governance and counter to your mission. It doesn't take any more money to set the expectations with your SOC staff and provide a positive or at the very least not a negative experience with the employees at your company.

Providing professional services with courtesy along with being timely and accurate, will build trust. This trust translates into more people coming to you for help, reporting suspicious activity and more people following policy. Not all services can be handled through the SOC, but with a little thought and effort, most daily employee interactions can be easily handled by your SOC staff.

SET THE EXPECTATIONS

The key to customer service is setting expectations. If you allow walk-ins to get new employee badges, it is possible you will occasionally have a waiting line. Find out what your average wait time is and make sure to publicize that fact. Think of your own experiences. If you knew that the average wait time for an oil change was 20 minutes on the weekend, you would be happy if it was faster and irritated if it took a lot longer. Twenty-five minutes is not out of line, but 60 minutes is. You still need your oil changed, so you wait, but you are not satisfied.

We worked for a company where the security department was responsible for background checks. As part of the on-boarding process, we got a lot of complaints that the checks took too long and cost too much. The hiring managers also had no way to get a status on an applicant, they just had to wait until they got notified of the pass/fail.

In 2000, as part of our shared services organization, all employees were surveyed as to the level of their satisfaction with our service. The survey only went out to managers and above. It was the first time they had ever been asked about how they felt with regard to the jobs we did in corporate security, and they let us have it. Only 59% responded that they were satisfied or very satisfied with our performance. There were also 27 pages of comments.

It was difficult reading through the comments. In corporate security, we saw ourselves as protectors of the company assets and people. We had solved thefts, walked people to their cars late at night in bad neighborhoods, helped resolve stalking and sexual harassment issues, and many more things that most employees probably never even heard or thought about. We didn't expect to get a big old pat on the back, but the venom in some of the comments was hard to read.

We had a meeting and we vented and then we got over it. Mostly.

Then we did what the rest of the shared services organization was doing. We sorted the comments into groups of similar concerns and picked the top three items and started the difficult task of figuring out how we could make those pain points either cheaper or faster or less painful. We used a management system similar to Six Sigma and performed root cause analysis after creating process maps for ever service we provided. The biggest gripe was around those background checks. The first clue we had that the frustration may be justified was that no one in the department knew what the average turnaround time even was. We measured it. The average time was 14 days. The clocks started once we received the form from the applicant and we knew some were taking more than a week to fill it out. There was speculation that the delay was intentional since we also required a drug test, but all of this was hidden from the hiring leader. All they know was that it sometimes took a month to clear a new hire and only then could they start work.

After a lot of work, we reduced the average time to 3.4 days and managed negotiate with a new vendor to get the price reduced by around $20 per screening. That was a great piece of work and a true team effort, but it would have been all for nothing if we had failed to let our customers know. Communication was definitely the key. We told our customers the results of the survey and what we were committing to improve. Then we told them the facts many times in many formats. In a big email, as part of our annual security awareness training, as a separate paper flyer (it was 2004), and in our SLAs that were reporting to all of the business unit leaders and posted on our website. We also made sure to remind them right before the next annual survey of what they had asked for and what we had done. We even went so far as to automate the hiring process and make sure every hiring leader got an email with our commitment to turnaround the screening within 5 days.

It took a couple of years, but when we started hearing people talk about new hires and that it would take about 5 days, we knew we had communicated effectively. It had become an accepted part of our company culture and common knowledge for anyone who hired staff. In 5 years, our score went up to 92% of the people surveyed that either agreed or strongly agreed that we provided a valuable service. That 92% was the highest in shared services, even higher than HR.

MISTAKES WILL HAPPEN—OWN THEM, FIX THEM, FOLLOW UP, AND MOVE ON

Let's discuss mistakes. Regardless of how competent the staff is or how clearly you've communicated the expectations, either mistakes are going to occur, or people will believe that mistakes have occurred and it is not useful to argue. Over the years, we've worked with all kinds of vendor doing new construction, retrofits, upgrades, and repairs in all types of terrain and environmental conditions. What worked on a vehicle gate in the panhandle of Texas, may not work in the northern reaches of North Dakota. Sometimes the issues that cropped up were our fault and sometimes they were the vendors. Watching different vendors react to mistakes that were made helped us develop a philosophy that translated into how we wanted to be perceived. What we learned was that regardless of skill or experience, stuff just happened. Mistakes were not daily occurrences, but they were common enough. What made me want to work with one vendor over another, was how that company reacted when the mistake was identified. The best companies didn't point fingers or even waste time with excuses. They identified the problem, owned it, and moved heaven and earth to make it right.

Since no one forces a vendor to take work, and they do have the choice of walking away, we made sure that if we owned part of the fault, that we made it right not just financially, but also with being flexible. This is what being a strategic partner really is about. We met regularly and discussed open issues and decided how to deal with them. Since we already worked closely and communicated regularly, mistakes were more rare. But when they cropped up, we dealt with it together and made it right, then we moved on to the next project.

That is the same approach we used in the SOC. The customers we had the most interaction with, we set up a monthly meeting. When we made an error, we owned it and put in extra effort to make it right. We did not get walked all over. We did also hold the business accountable when they were in error, but we never abused our authority. In this way we earned their respect and increased our credibility. Having said that, there are always politics involved in corporations. Occasionally, a situation would come up where a very senior person in the business became dissatisfied with an interaction they'd had with the SOC. Even after we'd made it right, there was a small majority of people who wanted retribution. We mentioned in another chapter that we had much higher than normal retention for our contact SOC operators. High isn't 100% though and we did lose at least one person per year. On more than one occasion, when a VP wanted blood, we may have inferred that we removed the operator in question, even though the person who left wasn't even working on that shift. It was useful and we felt a harmless ruse that satisfied the VIP while protecting our workers who had done nothing wrong.

A strange and unplanned side effect of all our communications, which centered around people's interaction with the SOC, was that people didn't realize that we had an actual security department. In meetings, when people found out we were in security they would ask if we worked for the SOC. At first, we were put off, but upon reflection, for the average employee we saw no harm. We have online anonymous IRs and a process with attribution as well. Anyone could call the SOC and report whatever the issue was and it would get routed to the right person. No longer did people have to call several numbers or email a bunch of us trying to figure out who they needed help from. The SOC was a true one-stop shop and while the corporate security department did so much more, that work was not directly in support of the average employee on a day-to-day basis.

Since the SOC is such a natural fit as the face of security, you need to make sure that you emphasize customer service in your training and in your performance management. When it comes to security, the customer may not always be right, but they are always the customer. The daily habit and attitude that your staff must take is that of customer service and support. SOC operators need to be professional, courteous, and helpful. They also need to know that you support them. Every SOC we have run has audio recording on all the phone lines. We inevitably got complaints and we investigated them all. If we discovered that the SOC operator was out of line, we would handle it with coaching and if necessary discipline. However, if we discovered that the employee had been abusive or out of line, it was standard practice for us to send the audio clip to them and copy their manager. That usually ended the issue. Quickly.

Starting a SOC from scratch as we did twice so far in our careers, is a transition for any company. We realize that two instances do not reach statistical significance. However, we feel that the results we experienced, while not guaranteed, are repeatable. Over time, employees get used to calling the SOC when they have issues and when those issues are competently resolved, employees tend to rely on that service. Many times we have had people call upper management and have a great experience working with a specific operator and from then on ask for that operator specifically. We are not going to claim that all of our operators were equal in capability or charisma, but getting to the day shift is earned. Only on day one of training did operators start on days without proving they were the best, so different employees locked on to different dayshift operators based on their first contact, not realizing that all of them were equally competent.

SOC performance doesn't get the rest of the department off the hook of course, but the idea is to build a strong SOC and make sure that even if the entire company knows about all the department members and what job they perform (highly unlikely), that they also know that the initial touch point for all things security is the SOC, especially if it's 24/7. To assist further, make sure the phone number is easy to remember and plastered everywhere. One place is not enough. When we were first raising awareness, we printed up small stickers with the SOC number and in case of emergency and put them under the handsets of every phone we could get to at corporate headquarters. When we visited remote sites we spread them around every chance we got. Our numbers were all over our company's intranet and the operators were instructed to have the employees call us directly instead of just forwarding on the call so they would learn it. We even printed it on the back of everyone's badge.

Before we started these awareness campaigns and integrated ourselves into the company's cultural consciousness, people would routinely question the worth of the security department and most especially the SOC. Once we became a part of the fabric of the company and included in so many different processes that the company became reliant on the SOC, people stopped asking those questions. We were viewed as truly necessary because we had actively worked to making ourselves that way. It wasn't just that people no longer questioned our value, it was that we had worked hard to provide so many valuable critical services at a cost lower than any out sourced alternative could have and we did it with such a strong customer focus, that we couldn't be replaced for a lower cost provider without losing essential services or capabilities.

HISTORICAL LESSONS

When we first heard that we would not only be measured, but that a portion of our pay raise and bonus would depend on our customer service score, we were horrified. Of all the shared services organizations, we were voted the least huggable. We had just upgraded the card access system with a suspicious new technology (proximity badges) and most employees were convinced that we were able to track them anyway, as if the proximity badge had GPS technology. At one company we had a union shop and from time to time, we were responsible for getting a union worker terminated for theft or some other code of conduct violation. Not many people were fans, and the first overall score of 59% was about what I expected.

As we mentioned earlier, there were also quite a few pages of verbatim comments that were hard to read. Twenty plus years of irritation and downright anger flowed into those paragraphs. We could have handled it any number of ways, and it was tempting to get defensive and ignore them. For some of the comments, that is exactly what we did. The survey was truly anonymous and a minority of people let the hate flow through them. However, most of the comments, while critical, were specific and similar to others. After we vented and calmed down, we got busy putting all of them into groups. We identified around 10 areas of dissatisfaction. Since that is way too many to tackle, we opted to target to top three. We had around one hundred comments. Nearly 20 were not made for prime time and were disregarded. Nearly half fell into the top three concerns and the rest broke down into smaller clusters until the tenth concern had three comments.

Once we knew what to focus on, the next step was to set up interviews with people in the business units who were willing to talk about the issues. We brought the top three concerns and an open mind and the weirdest thing happened. The managers we spoke with wanted to talk to us. They agreed about the pain points and were willing to tell us why there were such areas of concern and even help us brainstorm on ways to address the issues. They were also skeptical that we would change anything, since nothing had ever changed.

It was an epiphany for us. No one had ever asked the business if they were happy with the services that they, through the corporate overhead, paid for. Once asked, they had plenty to say. Our concern was that they would find some way to either get rid of the services or outsource them, but if we had never asked for feedback and then put effort into improving the problem areas, that is exactly what would have happened. We never thought of the business as the enemy, though from our experience, we knew about 2% of any company is either stealing something or doing something they shouldn't. We rarely received cooperation to solve those cases, so it became easy to make the relationship adversarial. But when we started to view the business as not just customers, but partners, everything worked better including investigations. What we saw over time was a drop-in theft at the sites. Our improved relationships led to site security improvements, which increased accountability. With the new surveillance and video monitoring systems we had put in place, we tackled one of the pain points, copper theft, by conducting regular video site checks at the most at-risk locations during the night when the majority of these thieves would strike. Once we caught a few thieves in the act of breaking in or stealing from the yard, dispatched police and the bad guys were caught. That word gets around in the criminal world. We not only increased the good will of local management and faith of upper management, we also instilled the belief that we would catch whoever did the stealing and all loss decreased.

It never occurred to us that measuring and working to improve customer satisfaction would improve the security posture, but that is exactly what happened.

CHAPTER 17

Metrics

INTRODUCTION

We were involved in a merger at one company where the new CEO stated that if you couldn't measure it, you shouldn't be doing it. At the time, that was not a comforting message for a corporate security department. It was 2000, and we tried to benchmark with other companies, but what we found was that few had any metrics and the few that existed were a bit anemic. Metrics are more commonplace today than they were in 2000, but for a traditional security department, it was an odd concept to consider.

INCIDENT REPORTS

The first reaction was incredulity. The first metric we all thought of was around what we called incidents. An incident could be a lot of things, but most started with a call from an employee somewhere in the company to report something they thought we should be aware of or handle, like a missing piece of equipment or damage to company property or perhaps hunters trespassing. Some were false or just misunderstandings and some were very real and needed to be investigated and have some action taken. The concern was that we would be held accountable for reducing the number of incidents once we reported how many occurred. We all knew there were actions we could take to help reduce the number slightly, but most required spending money on some form of security system, and at the time we didn't have a capital budget. We could only recommend that a facility add cameras, card readers, and alarms, and then it was up to them to budget for them. The problem was that compared to the operational needs of the facility, the security project was always at the bottom of the list and the first to be cut when they either didn't get all the budget they requested or when they were given a budget challenge mid-year.

Spoiler alert. Eventually, we used the data gathered along with criminal metrics in neighborhoods to justify the installation of new security equipment.

161

Security Operations Center Guidebook. DOI: http://dx.doi.org/10.1016/B978-0-12-803657-0.00017-9

We were initially worried that the statement about metrics was a way to eliminate or reduce the security department, but in fact, it gave us the data we needed to build a business case to not only increase security spend, but to also centralize the security budget and give control of the spend and prioritizing to the director of corporate security.

Metrics by themselves are useless. Only by evaluating the quality and the detail of the metrics you gather can they become tools to improve your operations.

As we've discussed, a SOC can range from a very basic operation all the way up to becoming the central nervous system of the entire corporation. The more services it provides the more metrics you can come up with. Before we dive in too deep on metrics though, let's do some level setting.

TYPES OF METRICS

A metric is simply a way to measure a thing. Let's say you are a new security director and your new company has a SOC. They do a lot of stuff and seem very busy, but you have no optics into what that stuff is. The first thing to do is just to capture all the activity.

Initially, if you ask for data, you may get something like this for a typical month: 1000 alarms. Programmed access for 50 badges. Generated 30 reports. Answered 500 calls. Reviewed 200 hours of recorded video.

In this form, these are definitely metrics because they are groups of stuff that was done. This is not performance applied, just a bunch of stuff that represents how the SOC operators spent most of their time. The data also lacks specificity. It isn't actionable. Let's drill down into alarms.

They received 1000 alarms in a month. Why? What type? When it comes to alarms, there are three basic types, valid, false, and nuisance. A valid alarm is a legitimate alarm condition. Someone somewhere either opened a door with a key or forced it open illegally. The alarm functioned as it was designed and the person is either an employee who is violating policy or someone breaking the law. For those who have been in corporate security for a while, you know that these alarms events are very rare and are in danger of being ignored due to the other two types.

A false alarm is one that is either programmed incorrectly or the programming is wrong. For instance, if you set up a door contact to go into an alarm condition of it is held open for more than a few seconds, but you set it up to alarm during normal business hours, you have a false alarm. It may make sense to set this up during hours when workers are normally not there, but it is a waste of time to set it up during business hours. Another type would be in the wiring, which was done incorrectly, and you got an alarm event when someone performed a normal exit through a door. If the vendor and SOC coordinate during the installation of a new or replacement card access system, both of these should be avoided. Simply asking the people onsite, especially daytime workers when the building is considered closed for business, is often not enough. Most people forget the cleaners and some buildings are subject to afterhours work that may be inconsistent. Make sure you know when the building is considered truly empty before you set up your time zones. Also, require the vendor to perform a commissioning with your SOC operators that test each alarm point and card reader in all conditions to ensure that the wiring is correct.

A nuisance alarm is more rare, but an example would be a door contact on a garage door of a buildings dock that is located in an area where storms or strong winds shake the door enough to cause an alarm condition. The alarm is programmed correctly and installed properly, but it is the nature of garage doors that they are not sealed tight. Similarly, there are some window alarms that also go off under similar conditions. Having them sensitive enough to detect and actual forced entry may require that you deal with the occasional nuisance. Still, it is a good idea to pull up the cameras that cover these areas to make sure something isn't actually going on.

If the SOC only reported the total number of alarms without any context, you would get a report that said you had 1000 alarms every month. That might make it seem to someone in your company that there were 1000 break-ins. That would be an epidemic. And if you had 1000 and 999 were false, how could your SOC possibly catch the 1 real one? They would be trained to hit the button to clear the other 999. The 1000 number is also misleading because 500 of them may be from the same door, especially if there is a problem with the wiring or programming. Without the detail of how many physical devices are responsible for the 1000 alarms, it's impossible to take any action.

Without drilling down and identifying the problem door and then digging in to see what's really happening, you will never fix anything. This requires someone to be onsite and working with someone in the SOC. This doesn't have to cost a lot. In fact we don't recommend calling a vendor until you understand exactly what's going on. This also speaks to the level of maturity of your SOC. If all your operators do is follow a procedure for each alarm event and never even pay attention to let alone diagnose a problem, then they lack maturity or perhaps good training and guidance. Your operators should feel as if they own the systems. The alarm contacts usually have two states, either open or closed. You don't want your SOC staff to be as robotic.

PHONE STATS

Another great metric for analyzing your SOC operations are the types of calls that are coming in. Simply recording 500 incoming calls doesn't tell the story. You need to require your operators to code the calls. Many businesses have call centers and are already paying for software that allows for coding and reporting, and if yours doesn't, the price for this type of software is reasonable. You may find that you have between 3 and 5 types of calls that account for 99% of the volume, with the last bit being identified as other. Training a simple diagram by the phone will remind the operators which button on the phone to push for each type of call. After that, you will have an actionable report. The result may reflect what you expected for a well-run SOC, or they may point out problems. Perhaps they show a higher than expected number of people requesting access changes. Why do so many people not have the access they need? It could be that your initial profile is too restrictive or perhaps people are asking for access they really don't need, but simply want. Regardless of the reason, with a little investigating and some root cause analysis, you can come up with a game plan to address the issue. This should result in the reduction of this type of call.

If you've never gathered metrics before, you may find that it is very labor-intensive initially. We started with spreadsheets. It may sound odd, but one of the first metrics we tracked was how much time we spent tracking metrics. If you guessed that we used that data to purchase some software to help automate the collection of metrics, you'd be right. The less labor-intensive and more automatic you make it, the more accurate and usable your data will be and the less your staff will hate you.

Don't forget to tell your entire department why you are gathering all this data and also to remind them how you have been able to improve operations by using the data. Telling new employees is important of course because they may come from a company where they don't track anything and it may seem odd or a waste of time, but it's also important to remind long-term employees how the data is used to justify the very existence of the department and of course, all of its workers.

PERFORMANCE METRICS

Performance metrics are everyone's favorites, and the cause for our original concern. We feared that once the metric of X number of incidents was reported up the chain, we would be hit with a goal of reducing that number by X percent. Since even we didn't understand the causes of all the incidents, we were sure that upper management would come up with some random and unachievable goal. There are all kinds of people, some reasonable and some not so much, so our concerns were realistic, but thankfully not justified. Like most departments we were given a goal around budget. We were allowed to come up with other measures on our own, at least initially and they required us to support them.

In an earlier chapter we covered customer service and used the example of on boarding, specifically background checks and how long it took us to complete them. When it came to metrics, here was a goal that we found we could improve and because it was so important, it remained a goal we kept long after we squeezed all the performance out if it we could. The first year, we had a goal to analyze the issue and come with a plan of action. The second year, we set a goal to reduce the average turnaround time from 14 to 5 days. This was based on the data we came up with through our process improvement work. It was not some random guess, but a supportable and achievable goal as a simple average. It was still a little nerve wracking until we proved it, but over time we actually averaged 3.4 days through continuous improvement.

If your company is reasonable around goal setting, they should allow you to gather data the first year on any measurement and to perform some type of root cause or process management analysis. This is often called a baseline. Some companies have integrated Six Sigma into their management structure and this is a very common practice, in others it may take some convincing. The pressure to come up with goals around performance may put you into a situation where you are just guessing at what a reasonable or stretch target would be. If that happens and it's clear that you can't make it, then make use of the time by getting hard data to explain why and work toward a more achievable goal.

SERVICE LEVEL AGREEMENTS

SLAs are a type of performance metric or goal that you set up within your company, usually with the business units. It should come as no surprise that as a security department, you are identified as overhead. The worst term we were called was a burden. Having your budget called "Burden," right on the spreadsheet you get from finance is a motivation killer, but it's no joke. Language is powerful, and having the business units calling all groups that don't make revenue burdens, is not the basis of a healthy relationship, especially when there are services that must be performed because of either regulatory or contractual requirements. The kindest thing we were ever called was a "Necessary Evil." We focused on being necessary and being able to prove it.

The first SLA we came up with was the 5-day turnaround time, but also that the average cost would not exceed $140 per screening. When we evaluated the process, we found that we were being charged an average of $170 per background check and that the contract was essentially an evergreen, or with no end date. The vendor just had income they didn't need to work for. To be fair, there had also been a hiring freeze for many years and that ended, so the ability to negotiate both with multiple vendors and at a higher volume, made getting a cheaper rate easier.

Another SLA that we had was around the time it took for the SOC to answer a call. We set a target for all calls to be answered within 5 seconds. Initially we made that easily, but over time, as our credibility grew and so did the range of services we offered, the call volume increased to a point where we either had to add an additional dayshift operator or increase our wait time. Thanks to tracking all the other metrics in the SOC, we had the justification we needed to add a third operator weekdays from 8:00am to 4:00pm, our busiest hours for customer interaction. And how did we know that? You guessed it, our call tracking software.

When we started tracking metrics, we first used spreadsheets, but the fact is we first had to use paper and pen and then type the info into a spreadsheet at the end of each shift. Those were dark days and rumors of mutiny were rampant. Whether you are being forced to start using metrics, or you simply think it would be beneficial, try to get automated tools in place from the beginning. In our case, we found that we could use the call center's tools for free. It was easy to implement and only required a little training and we had reports that would slice and dice the data anyway we wanted. We set specific goals around hold times since no customers like to wait for someone to answer the phone, especially if you are corporate world's version of 9/11. Most card access systems have ok reporting, but getting the data out can be manually intensive. We used crystal reports to extract the data and because our company already had enough licenses, this was also a no-cost improvement that just required some initial training.

The metrics gathered can be used to measure and then improve performance. They can also be used to support business cases for acquiring additional resources. After 9/11, we were required to conduct security assessment of several types of critical facilities. We developed and risk assessment methodology internally and then went to local sites, both critical and noncritical, and conducted the assessments. The goal was not only to improve the assessment process by testing our core assumptions, but also to determine how many hours were required to conduct the assessments. By the number of critical sites we had as determined by a couple of different new regulatory requirements, we knew that we would need some new employees in order to perform all the work. The question was, how many?

We measured how long it took to conduct an assessment and multiplied that by the number of sites we had that required assessing. High critical sites required an assessment every year, medium every two and low every three. With this requirement, even if we only had 10 high critical sites, we would likely end up doing at least 30 every year based on how often each was required to be conducted. We also had to factor in the additional workload the same people performed and we had years of data to support those duties. Eventually, we had a business case for adding a total of five new people.

Hopefully by this point you are not still wondering why you should care about metrics. We admit it is not the sexiest of subjects. However, one of the chief complaints of any overhead organization is that they don't get the budget they need to meet their objectives. There are two things that every security department needs in order to get more budget love. The first is credibility and the second is credibility. Credibility is earned over time. To get there you need to first know what's happening in your company and why. Then you need to commit to performing at a certain level and then consistently meeting those expectations. Finally, you need to be able to function as a business professional, not just a security expert. You do this by responsibly using what resources you are given and being able to make business cases supported by data.

HISTORICAL LESSONS

We have given a lot of historical context to this subject, so we thought we would deviate just a little bit and discuss management expectations when it comes to metrics. Security departments have a habit of moving around. While at one company, we reported to facilities, safety, HR, and shared services. It is very likely that whoever you report to doesn't know a lot about security and will be biased based on their interactions with security over the years. Each time we had a new boss, we were always surprised by what they did and didn't care about.

We had been publishing our metrics monthly as well as quarterly and annually for a few years when we were instructed to change the term "escort." We had been providing an escort for employees to their cars in the parking lots as an afterhours service for years at our HQ. That portion of downtown Minneapolis has a high crime rate and the ramp most people used was a bit dark and creepy at times. Our new manager felt awkward discussing these escorts as she thought they implied something sexual. We eventually came up with a less suggestive term.

The same VP was also shocked to find out that as we introduced the SOC to the new Colorado and Texas regions, that the number of reported incidents grew. We had baseline numbers from the facilities department that previously had security responsibility without having any security people on staff.

When I warned her that the volume would likely increase until it matched what we were seeing in the north, she was shocked. It never occurred to us that she would take the baseline as an accurate representation what was happening. The reality was that they had nothing like the SOC. Not even a specific number to call to make reports, let alone any security awareness so people knew where to call. The managing director who was briefly in charge of the security department came from the southern region and claimed that they weren't a den of thieves like the north.

A year after the merger, that managing director was gone and McCoy was handed a stack of paper incident reports that the facilities admin had been keeping in a drawer. Even without a clear process to report, there was an impressive pile of activity. Once we advertised the SOC in the south and they went through our annual security awareness training, the number of reported incidents did come to close to equaling the reports from the north. Our mistake was not explaining this to upper management. It seemed so obvious to us, that it never occurred to us to bring it up. That was a lesson worth remembering. You can't control what your upper management cares about or even retains, but you do control the message to give them. Always be ready to explain variances from the norm, both positive and negative, and if you believe something is going to happen based on your experience, then report it and make sure to differentiate between the fact and your opinion. When it does come to pass, they will remember your prophetic predictions and that will only increase your credibility as a security professional.

CHAPTER 18

Developing Partnerships

INTRODUCTION

It may be possible to successfully run a SOC and even a security department without any partners in the business and community, but it is a lot easier getting positive work done with the other company departments and community groups working with your SOC rather than against without them. Developing strategic partnerships takes time and often a large amount of patience. Seek counsel from your peers within the industry because you will never cease to learn from others who are doing things a different way.

START FROM WITHIN

The first place to seek out partners are within your own reporting structure. Corporate security departments probably have the widest variety of reporting relationships and get moved around more than any other department. We have been a part of security departments that have reported to a VP of sourcing, VP of HR, VP of facilities, the general counsel, the CFO, and even the VP of safety. Reorganizations occur and reporting structures change, but in each instance, we found ourselves paired up with other leaders of departments that we benefited in partnering with. Reporting to the same boss is an icebreaker for a conversation about what you can do for each other. If it's you breaking the ice, you would do better thinking about what you would like and what you can offer even before you ask for the meeting. Whether you are naturally introverted or extroverted, it's important to remember that it isn't critical to build lasting friendships with everyone in order to be successful. Minimally, what you need is professional respect and the ability and desire to assist each other in meeting your goals.

THE MOST OBVIOUS PARTNERS—SAFETY AND FACILITIES

Natural partners are certainly safety and facilities, but corporate security and in some way even more so, the SOC can offer services to every department in

Security Operations Center Guidebook. DOI: http://dx.doi.org/10.1016/B978-0-12-803657-0.00018-0

the company. You can function as intake for requests or initiating some process of documenting a safety concern or reporting a broken elevator to facilities. As an example, we have helped the safety department by taking in all of the company vehicle accident reports for the whole company. We created a separate 800 phone number and had it routed into the SOC so it would still get recorded, then the safety department made up key chains with the phone number to call to report the accident and made everyone across all locations use the SOC for reporting. The safety department could never staff a 24/7/365 phone, and paying a third party for such a service averaged around $50 K at the time.

This partnership had multiple benefits. At first it just sounded like a lot of extra work since the operators had to fill out paperwork each time a call came in. For large companies with thousands of vehicles, a hundred accidents a year is low. Not all were life threatening, many were small but all needed to be reported for insurance purposes. The first benefit was that we were able to claim cost savings. While $50 K doesn't sound like a lot considering labor for the SOC was around $750 K annually, it does add up over the years as a true benefit. One of the less tangible benefits was that our SOC could contact key management personnel if the employee was in a serious accident and perhaps a bit rattled. A third-party vendor would not know who to contact plus our employees liked talking to someone who was a part of the company.

The second benefit was that some of the accidents involved vehicle gates or other security equipment and we were notified right after it happened, speeding up our ability to restore operations. The third benefit was that since we helped save the safety department money, they were open to having one of our staff take up some of the time of their safety meetings to give face-to-face security awareness training and briefings. More communication is always better than a void, and getting face time with the line staff at those meetings had ongoing benefits and helped us build relationships with individuals at every location.

Another service we provided to the corporate safety department was being able to help them correct a finding they received from OSHA about material safety data sheets (MSDS) not be available to employees at times the local network was down. Safety provided a compact disc with the latest MSDS library to the SOC and with that the SOC was able provide MSDS to staff in the field or at locations via fax or reading the MSDS to the employee over the phone.

With facilities, your SOC could be their call tree dispatch for their site operations. Employees could call your SOC to inform them of facility issues such as lights out, elevators not working or other similar facility issues and the

SOC is then responsible for reporting that to the proper facility contact to get the issue resolved. It is important to track these things for your metrics because this is a work that ought to be measured since you are providing a companywide service. Another service that is the most natural to partner with your SOC with facilities is the monitoring of various mechanical alarms such as hi-temperature freezer alarms, elevator failure alarms, backup generator low fuel alarms, and hi-temperature alarms for your data centers, and so on. The list is only limited by your imagination.

INFORMATION TECHNOLOGY (IT) DEPARTMENT

The IT department of your company can be a great partner because you are both dependent upon each other for success but mostly because your SOC is using their networks and infrastructure for all your cameras and alarm panel communications. They help you to keep everything communicating over the network properly and you help them control the access to their data closets and data server rooms. You need that friendship so that both groups can help protect both the physical security and cyber security of your organization. Often our SOC would be the ones to alert the IT department to a site outage when our SOC would call IT to ask if they have an outage at a location because the SOC had just lost cameras and access panels were no longer communicating. By alerting them to this outage they were able to take immediate action and get the issue resolved in a timelier manner.

At one company, the IT security department had a software that would send an email alert to our SOC with information stating that an authorized device had been plugged into this location. The SOC would then be responsible for dispatching the local security officer, security manager, or other responding person to locate the device and confiscate it until it could be determined that the device is business-safe and necessary to be plugged into the system. This happened quite a bit in the beginning that executive management agreed that USB devices should be banned and employees were no longer authorized to use personal USB devices.

At another company, the IT security department installed a PC with monitor in our SOC with a program that monitored the network 24/7 for penetrations and viruses. If a penetration attempt or virus alarm sounded on the monitor, the SOC was responsible for contacting the on-call IT security person to respond to the virus or penetration. That is all they did at first. When it was realized that getting an on-callIT security person moving during the midnight hours was sometimes difficult, IT security decided that some additional steps might need to be taken by a SCO to slow the attack. So the IT security department wrote up a few simple proactive procedures with quick easy steps they could use during the graveyard hours that the SOC could take while one SCO was calling the on-call IT security person to respond to the cyber-attack. This worked well until a new chief information security officer was hired and found it appalling that lowly knuckle dragging physical security people were supporting IT functions and ended the practice by hiring additional people at greater cost to the company.

LAW ENFORCEMENT AGENCIES AND OFFICERS

Law enforcement organizations are another group that just makes sense to partner with, but most departments struggle to break the ice. Frankly some companies don't have much to offer or even much need, but if you have a lot of facilities with property that people like to steal, you will be dealing with law enforcement anyway, so why not find a way to make it a partnership? You already have so much in common. You don't like being ripped off and they don't like criminals ripping off anyone.

In dozens of locations across dozens of counties and several states, we had installed new card access and camera systems. These locations had material that people were fond of stealing because it was easy money that was hard to trace. Most of the facilities were also remote and a lot of the material was in fences, so it was hard to alarm. We initiated a program where our operators would perform security tours using the cameras at the highest risk sites at night. It took a little time, but they got skilled at it and started catching bad guys in the act. They would zoom in and get good evidence and report the thefts to local police, sending stills and video of the crimes to the departments. After a year, the SOC was calling the dispatches of the police directly and coordinating the arrest of thieves in real time, going so far as to let the police in and direct them to back up a few feet because the criminal was under the truck just behind them. Not only is that just plain cool, but also when our SOC calls these departments, they respond right away because we've built the credibility necessary for a good partnership.

Our corporate headquarters at one company was in the downtown portion of the city, right on the edge of where bad meets slightly better. The SOC had a lot of cameras around the perimeter of the HQ and performed the same service over the radio with the local precinct with similar results. If someone was fleeing on foot and headed in our direction, it was common for an officer to call us over a radio they had provided and ask us to look for them and inform the police on their movements.

The benefits of these Law Enforcement Officer (LEO) partnerships vary by department, but overall, law enforcement was much more responsive when we called because they knew we screened out false or nuisance alarms and that it was likely that they would be able to make an arrest when they showed up. Thus, we also got additional support when we needed it. A few times, there were cases when an employee was being stalked and there was a significant danger of them being harmed or killed. We never had an issue getting a few extra patrols by our location, especially during shift change. Of course, having detailed loss metrics and being able to show that we were saving the company money by reducing that loss was a significant milestone.

Companies often call vendors strategic partners. This is a popular term coined by sourcing departments around 2002 that essentially meant, that the company spent a LOT of money with these specific vendors and it only made sense to have cordial discussion about how much the bill would be and how each party could put out more effort to resolve any issues. In return for reduced pricing for more transparent and predictable workload, both sides would have regular meetings to discuss any conflicts and commit to resolve them in a friendly fashion. In other words, they would become partners and not just ticket takers.

We saw the value in this right away, having had some rocky relationships with vendors in the past. In the physical security industry throughout the 20th century, vendors were not often trusted not treated well. Some of their reputation was earned and some of it was a result of the fact that security equipment was becoming more technical and computer-dependent. Many of the corporate security departments lacked the skills necessary for basic project management, let alone have the technical skills to even know what to ask for beyond "make it work." The PSP certification from ASIS International that came out in 2004 was created to address this short coming. Prior to that, the only way a company could gain those skills was to either hire a former installer or send one of their employees through installation training and just gain experience over time.

VENDORS—YES, VENDORS TOO

Partnerships with vendors are similar to any other relationship. To be successful, you need to make working together if not pleasant, then at least less painful. The pain points for most vendors are; getting paid late for work performed, poorly defined scope, scope creep, rescheduling installation last minute, not having anyone who either knows how to program the equipment ahead of time and not allowing them access to do it themselves or basically working with an unorganized group that can't define what they want.

When you build that credibility and trust by working a few installations successfully, the potential benefit is better and lower cost designs and more responsive service calls. At one point I thought we had reached a level of partnership that, based on my benchmarking with peers, was unprecedented and the envy of many. But then we turned it up to 11 by getting the vendor to agree to carry very specific items in all of their service trucks. We had three years of data and had analyzed all of our service calls. After we had created a troubleshooting guide for our SOC operators, we had got to the point that we could reliably predict what was wrong at a remote location. That along with the list of most often broken or failing parts gave us a list of usual suspects, one of which was a control panel. It's a bigger ticket item and the vendor was initially loath to include it in their trucks. They offered speedy delivery but in some locations, that could still take a week and there was always the possibility of a manufacturing back order.

Even with properly installed lighting protection systems, due to the nature of our industry, we could still lose control panels due to strikes. As we had 3 years' worth of data and had built up trust, we were able to convince them to carry our requested load out. Having the SOC properly diagnose the problem also saved us an initial service call just to do the same thing. In the days before we adopted this change, a service truck would drive out (a 4- hour minimum charge plus mileage outside a certain radius), spend time figuring out the problem, and then coming back a few days later to fix it. Instead, we called them out and let them know what was wrong and they had the parts to fix the issue the first time. This resulted in an annual savings of around $10,000. Not a fortune, but nothing to sneeze at. More importantly, it resulted in sites being more secure and fixing issues faster, which made the site managers happier, which in turn increased our customer satisfaction numbers. It's all connected and it all works together to make a smoother, cheaper, and more effective service that some people love and most at least don't resent.

Other companies are also important partners, especially within your own industry. Nonindustry partners within your major operational regions are also beneficial and should not be ignored. All corporations want you to benchmark, and there always seems to be a new initiative that requires getting data from other companies. Being a trusted source of data will ensure more timely and eager cooperation in return. Security associations such as ASIS International are a good place to start, especially locally, but most industries also have industry committees for security. It is well worth the time and occasional travel dollars to build these relationships. The company not only gains from the shared security information, but also because our group was so strong, we often acted as the conduit for other departments to share data and benchmarks. We had a good network, but not all the other groups did.

You don't have to be a natural charismatic networker to form these partnerships. You only need to put some time into thinking about what you need, what your company needs, and what you can offer to provide a value-added service. In some cases, it also takes the patience to wait until the need arises so you don't have to make what can essentially be a cold call without purpose beyond maybe needing to work together at some point in the future.

It is also important that you build the partnerships at different levels. For instance, with the vendor example, we knew the vendor management but only knew a few of the installers, and not very well, but the SOC operators worked with the service technicians and installers often and they built trust and synergy. We also had different people at the vendor company whom we worked with regularly who would do the liaison for us and while we may have known everyone by sight, having that trust built at multiple levels of management and staff made for a much stronger and long-lasting partnership with the vendor.

HISTORICAL LESSONS

Of all the partnerships, the one that was most crucial to our success early on was the one with our vendor. We have described some of it already, but it is worth giving an example of something that we believe would not have happened if we hadn't built that trust and mutual respect.

After a large merger, the president of one business unit (the guy in charge of all plants), decided that since they had not used guards in the southern region where he came from, we didn't need to use them in the north either. At that company, our fiscal year was the calendar year, so January 1 was the first day of the fiscal year. We were told on September 10 that by the end of the fiscal year, all the guards working at the power plants in the northern region would be removed. This would create a savings of approximately $1.2 million in the first year and over the next 10 years come in at around $14 million. Part of the merger required a promise to save $100 million over the first 10 years, and we were just given responsibility for 14% of that number. There was a rumor that the removal of the guards was done on our orders, so if we could tell anyone, VP or higher, what to imagine what employees thought at the sites. That fact is that we argued vehemently against the security officers and countered with a proposal to staff the gates during the peak daytime hours and have the SOC run them afterhours. It was turned down with extreme prejudice.

We had just 2 weeks to design and price automating security at 7 plants across 3 states. Work began on October 1, and included automating access control of all the vehicle gates and adding additional card readers, cameras, lighting, and miles of fencing. This was not a warm climate install such as Texas, or even mild Colorado, this was in Minnesota, South Dakota, and

Wisconsin, so the winter cold and snow was coming down upon us very soon. The vendor had limited crews and couldn't perform simultaneous installations at all seven sites. The ground can and did start to freeze in November that year and there were also miles of trenching to be done and most of the installations were outside. If we had done what most companies did and just hand off the orders to a security company that we barely took the time to know, we would have failed. If over the previous years, we had soured our relationship with them or the internal installation crews that we needed to install the fencing and conduit, we would not even have some close to finishing the project on time. Some of the installations required us to come up with completely new ways of connecting cameras and card readers over long distances too great to trench and longer than was supported over twisted shielding copper pairs. But we had a strong association with that vendor who was not afraid to communicate with us because we developed that relationship of trust and flowing ideas.

In the end, we tested out and approved the last reader on December 28, 2 days early. We were also a tad under budget, which was a major feather in the cap for the security department. There is no way we could have accomplished this had we not already become real partners. We worked together as a team and dealt with each setback that came our way together. We still have mixed feelings about the project because we believe that a combination of security officer and technology provides the best security, but it was a remarkable accomplishment.

CHAPTER 19

Brand Awareness

INTRODUCTION

Security awareness is a part of a good security program. It says so in many books and it is true. But why is it true? Most regulations that cover security have some requirement for security awareness training at least annually. Some companies make their own and others buy videos from companies and show them. Some companies have a quiz at the end of the training to make sure employees were paying attention. But what is the actual goal? Is it to check off a box for an auditor by showing them your 100% completion of training? Is it even to get all the employees in your company to remember at least 80% of the security policy one day a year?

We would argue that the real purpose of security awareness is to get employees to be a little more aware of what is happening around the work place every day of the year and if they see some violation of security policy, that they recognize the security violation and either know immediately who to call without having to think about it, or that they know exactly where to find the phone number or email of your SOC who they need to report the security violation incident to.

ONE-STOP SHOP

Hoping that a huge percentage of employees will meet these high expectations is perhaps naïve, but you really don't need to reach them all. You just need to reach enough of them that you have a few acutely aware people at every office location who know what to do. It also helps to keep the message simple and have only one phone number. The logical number for all employees to be told to call is your SOC. It is the place they call if they lost their badge or if the badge stops working. It's where they call if they need additional access. In other words, it's a place they already call and interact with people from the security department when no one has done anything

177

Security Operations Center Guidebook. DOI: http://dx.doi.org/10.1016/B978-0-12-803657-0.00019-2

wrong. For the employees to know who to call, how to call, and when, you need brand awareness.

WHAT IS YOUR BRAND?

Different brands mean different things to people, but in the last 50 years, branding has become a fast way for people to identify a product or service, then make and remember judgments about the type of things they want from that brand, and whether they like the that brand or want to avoid that brand altogether. Your SOC along with your corporate security team is a brand. Period. That is why having a good customer service experience with the employees and company locations is so critical. When people call the SOC, especially the first time, it's because they need something. They need answers, they need to know who the proper subject matter expert is within the company they need to talk to or perhaps their access card is not working properly. Likely they are under some pressure or stress and want someone to help them. They may not know what to expect. Perhaps they lost their badge and think they will be chastised. Perhaps they think they should already have access to an area and are a bit defensive or even angry. Either way, the SCO is going to resolve their problem, but it is how they do so that matters. It isn't enough to be competent. They must also treat the employee with professionalism, courtesy, and if needed, simply put them at ease and reassure them that either they or someone from the corporate security team is going to be able to help them. After all, these things happen.

We're not saying that if a person loses 10 badges in a year that someone shouldn't have a chat with them, but it shouldn't be the SOC and you shouldn't hold up getting them their latest badge as a form of punishment. Credibility is hard to earn and easy to lose. If you have a serious problem with many people losing badges, think about charging them if they lose more and each year. At least the person losing it is calling and reporting it right away. Do you really want them to put off making that call for a few days because they don't want to get in trouble?

THE SOC IS YOUR BRAND

The SOC needs to build and maintain trust. Employees need to feel comfortable calling them. This is how you build your brand. You don't tell them to trust you, you show them. But let's take a few steps back. First, you need to make sure your SOC is ready for prime time. That the operators are trained and that you are comfortable that they know not only what you want them to do but how you want them to do it. You should already have recruited people who have a customer service mindset and had a few mock calls during their training.

We have recorded every call in every SOC we've ever run. If we had not, we may not have believed what some of the SOC operators told us. We have both been in security management at all levels and we've seen and heard some offensive stuff, but it is still surprising what some people will say over the phone to what is essentially a coworker but somehow deemed a lesser person because they are "just taking phone calls." When people cross the line, the SOC manager or perhaps even the corporate security director needs to address the issue appropriately with management of the offender and/or HR, but no matter how mean someone becomes the operators should never lose their cool and strive to remain professional always.

ADVERTISING YOUR BRAND

Once you are sure you are ready for business, you need to come up with an advertising campaign. You must create the awareness that you have a new service. It is important to keep the message simple, especially at first. If you still have a different process for 911 calls at your main or remote locations, it is critical that you stress this in your communication plan. The employees need to know when not to call as much as they do when to call. Just a heads up in that one email, regardless of where it comes from, is not a communications plan.

Hopefully you have a communications department and they are interested in helping. We've dealt with very cooperative communication departments as well as some who felt it was their job to control all communication in the company including security awareness. Hopefully you have someone who is willing to help and not try to drive or even squash your plans, since it is your responsibility to get the word out.

You should not underestimate the importance of picking an easy-to-remember phone number for your SOC. You don't need to come up with some fancy logo or spend money on some fancy campaign, but you should communicate using different internal media and spread the message out over time. As stated earlier, we have printed up stickers with the SOC phone number and placed them on every phone with a clear message on who to call and when, so no one had to waste time looking it up which is critical in an emergency. We also printed the number on the back of every employee and contractor's badge and had the number added to the home page of the company's intranet. We even went so far as to send out a paper letter to every employee as part of our run up to our mandatory security awareness training, clearly listing the number and explaining when to call. We followed that up by including the same message in the actual online training and even added it to the in-person new employee orientation training.

ROME WAS NOT BUILT IN A DAY

Don't expect the entire company to hop on board the very first day or even in the first year. It takes time to build a new brand. Looking back at how integral our SOCs became to the daily operations after a few years, it's hard to remember a time when they didn't exist. Be patient and persistent, without making people avoid you in the halls for fear of hearing your pitch one more time. Provide a positive and valued service, and it will happen.

The benefits of a strong SOC brand will also become obvious over time. You will be better connected with sites and employees and more informed as to what is happening daily within your company. We predict that the number of reported incidents will go up a little your first year and even more in your second year. This is a common reaction to having more people aware that you exist and more importantly, how they can reach you and when.

One company experience made this clear. Our SOC was already established in the company when a merger was announced. The company we merged with didn't have a SOC or even a security department. The facilities department was the only place capable of handling security incidents, and we were assured as part of the merger integration process, that the new company didn't suffer from the same theft and harassment issues as ours. There were implications that our company had some systemic problem to have so many incidents being reported on an annual basis with their number being zero.

We were both younger then and naïve, but we were surprised at how upper management from both sides seemed to agree. Flash forward one year and we were given a pile of paper reports that had never been investigated. Flash forward by the end of the second year once the communication plan had time to take effect across the company, and the like-sized company that was now our southern region had almost identical numbers of incident reporting across all categories of incidents.

What this situation reinforced for us was that what we were doing worked and our earlier results were not a fluke. Awareness training may not be as large of a preventative as some claim, but when done properly, it does ensure that when things do occur, they are reported.

HISTORICAL LESSONS

We have used many examples at a couple of our companies that we have worked for together and separate from each other. We have learned a great deal from our time at each one of those companies and in some ways, that made starting over at one company harder. It was frustrating to start off with no credibility we both felt like banging our heads against the wall on multiple occasions. The corporate office (or Mother Ship as it was often called by the business units) was responsible for oversight. Before each of the locations had their inspection with a government agency for security compliance, members of our corporate security team went to each location and conducted security assessments to make sure they were ready. Some of our predecessors may have used and even scheduled these trips as mini vacations, wanting to go to some of the locations at times of the year when the weather was nice, regardless of when the inspection with the government agency was scheduled. Except for these interactions, the sites were very autonomous, using local vendors for alarm monitoring and in many cases managing their own card access systems, even though the access control system was an enterprise-wide system across the corporation. The idea of using, let alone relying on the Mother Ship to actually help a site security standing and provide good service was a hard message to sell.

Since our business case for creating the SOC relied on the savings created by taking over the monitoring from third-party vendors, we did have the leverage and the capital budget to make the changes. What we needed was some local cooperation. We picked a few early adopters willing to work with us and chose not to tackle the most vocal of business unit opposition at first. Slowly but surely, the SOC took over administrative control of the enterprise system along with the monitoring and card access programming for the majority of locations with the exception of those few sites with their own large guard force capable of monitoring locally. The managers for the sites reported up through each of their business units and had security leaders for each business unit. We sold our brand to them first and let each success spread within the business unit. When the more resistant managers heard from their peers that we took workload off their plates and provided not just the same services, but more services both quickly and competently along with a strong focus on customer service, the resistance slowly began to disappear, albeit grudgingly.

As predicted, it did take a couple of years from the moment we started operations, but building a brand is not a fast exercise. It requires patience, strong commitment to customer satisfaction with a willingness to take critical feedback, and then work to continuously improve the value added to the company. Since we had the luxury of having a security manager at every location as required by a government agency, our key customer base was smaller. But each site had its own security awareness training that corporate security supported and the SOC was there to support them. While we certainly had to address the needs of all employees, we had less day-to-day interaction with them because they could turn to local security resources. As time continued, the SOC with leadership from the corporate security team was involved in threat management teams, crisis management, mass notification, and providing a 24/7, 365 days a year, one-stop shop for answers to all things security, most especially access control. Email requests went from 1K a year to over 5K annually. Call volumes from customers went from less than 10K a year to close to 40K on an annual basis. Our brand was strong.

CHAPTER 20

Continuous Improvement

INTRODUCTION

You've done it. Congratulations. You wrote an impressive business case, designed a SOC that was just right for your company and then you hired good people and trained them into a cohesive SOC that has become the security nerve center of your corporation. Regulators and auditors love you because you have all the data on all of the controls they care about most at your fingertips. Time to relax and just enjoy your good standing, right?

Wrong! Ok, that was an obvious trap but you're still reading so we have that going for us. Now that you have your operation up and running you need to make sure that you don't rest on your laurels. The down side of measuring anything is that management will always want improvement. The reality is that there will come a point when even if you do everything possible, you won't be able to squeeze out any more. We think that is a long way off and should not be used as an excuse to try and so will your boss. What you need to do is show that you have evaluated all the aspects and that you can prove you have reached a point of diminishing returns.

PICK YOUR POINTS

What you want to do is make sure that you are ahead of the process that is so predictable, so don't get surprised. Instead anticipate the requests and have a plan ready. There are always items that can be categorized as low hanging fruit. It may be an overused expression, but that's likely because it seems to be a constant in business. Take any department in the company, and once you take a step back and spend time not just cranking on the day-to-day work product, but actually evaluating what could be improved, some obvious areas will stick out. It's likely that people in that department have known for some time, but if you only have four people doing the work of five or six, it's hard to find the time to figure out what needs to be improved, let alone how.

183

Security Operations Center Guidebook. DOI: http://dx.doi.org/10.1016/B978-0-12-803657-0.00020-9

Once those areas are tackled, focus on your pain points. If your company does perform customer satisfaction surveys that include comments, then you should have the ammo you need. If not, perform one just for security. Make sure you actually keep it anonymous or you will lose trust before you even have a chance to build it. Not all improvements will save money, some just reduce make work or allow you to do more with less. Finance is very particular about what it calls hard savings, so don't expect a lot of credit for cost avoidance, just make sure your boss understands the net benefit to the company.

GET A BLACK BELT OR BECOME ONE

When you have run out of suggestions from inside your department and other employee concerns, then use your company's resources. If your company is a Six Sigma or Lean shop, find a Black Belt and ask for an evaluation. If that resource is not available, consider getting a consultant, or better yet, get training in some form of management system. Six Sigma is perhaps the most well known, but they are certainly not the only game in town. Do your research and find a methodology that works for you.

If you reach a pace where you have convinced your upper management that you have exhausted improvement potential in your department, look to take on additional workload. When it comes to onboarding, most companies waste a lot of time, which delays people's start time or at a minimum, makes them ineffective while they wait for their technology and credentials. Each company is different, but if you have a SOC, it is likely that you own the provisioning and de-provisioning of physical access. If a full evaluation takes place that covers the entire process, from a headcount being approved in the budget process, all the way to a new worker becoming fully productive, most corporate or shared services departments have been involved. If the pressure is on, volunteer to spearhead a project to assess the entire process from end to end and come up with recommendations for reducing the overall time and fixing problems that exist with the process.

When you are on the quest for improvement, make sure that you and especially your staff don't get improvement fatigue. Make sure to let your folks know when they are doing a good job and never forget to celebrate milestones. Security departments often see the worst of their company's employees and certainly the worst from society. You have to be able to blow off steam in a healthy way that will not result in a call to HR or a car accident.

The only constant is change. Just as you must evolve and learn new skills over time or become a dinosaur, a SOC must also change over time to ensure that it remains a relevant and valuable asset to the company. A SOC is just a place where security work gets done for the company and as such it relies on technology and people. Both of these will fail from time to time. You may have heard that it takes 17 positive interactions to make up for a negative one. I don't doubt the ratio, but I do know that this ceases to be true if the negative interaction is truly an epic fail.

As with many things in life, consistency is the key. Your staff need to perform their tasks with precision and each interaction with a customer needs to be polite and most importantly, helpful. Getting to this point will take some time, but once achieved, you must work even harder to maintain. The concept of continuous improvement is not new, but there are an infinite number of ways to approach it. In Chapters 16 and 17 we covered customer service and metrics, respectively. Your customers will tell you what is important to them about security, but they will rarely tell anyone else. It is up to you to take that feedback and present it to the heads of the business units along with your plan on how you will improve on the areas that have received the worst feedback. Make sure to read carefully through the verbatim comments. Remember, these customers are employees. Many have been with the company for 20 plus years and while they are not security experts, they do know what they need to support their objectives. They also know the buildings they office and how it is used and misused by other employees better than you.

One mistake you should avoid is trying to tackle too many improvements at one time. Remember, the regular job of the SOC is challenging enough and if you have taken on additional tasks to show the value of the SOC, chances are your staff will not be bored. I recommend no more than three areas of focus and if possible only one, especially if there is a lot of dissatisfaction with the area that needs improvement. Don't just rely on a satisfaction score and a few verbatim comments when you are completing your improvement plan. Go out and meet with your key customers and conduct more in-depth interviews. Ask them straight out what they consider to be an acceptable level of performance.

Let's take something as basic as how long it takes to answer a call on average. By analyzing your trended data over time, you will know when your peak call times occur. Hopefully when it's slow, you aren't getting complaints about length of time to answer a call. Don't make assumptions about what your company's employees want. We did initially at one company and we were wrong. We felt it better to resolve each call to its completion, which lead to people calling in and listening to the phone ring for longer than they felt was reasonable. They felt it was better to have the line answered and notified that they would be put on hold that having the phone ring until a person was available. Company's cultures vary, but at Xcel, they knew we were busy, but they would rather have hold music and a phone ringing and not know if or when we would answer. That doesn't mean that they wanted to be on hold forever, in fact they were very clear about how long they were willing to wait on hold as well. But with that data, we were able to change how the SCOs handled calls. Of course we had a system in place that we got from our own customer call center that gave us detailed metrics about the time to answer, the length of time on hold, the length of time per call, and how long a person waited before they hung up.

We will caution you not to try and make operational changes based on outliers. Some of those may be very vocal, but you are there to serve the entire company, not one or two people. That is unless they are in your direct chain of command, then you might want to consider it. It also helps when you share the information back with your customers. They may have no idea for instance that you only have two people answering calls during the day and your call volume for an average dayshift is 640 calls.

Also, make sure to let your customers know that you worked on the thing they cared about the most and that you either achieved the target or at the very least that you made improvement in the area. It is far better to only commit to improving one area and then really nailing it, than to overpromise and fall short. Most of security is how people feel about it. The more competent you appear, the better.

The worst case is that you commit to improving an area and you fail. Failure happens. It never stops sucking, but it will happen sooner or later. The worst thing you can do is to get defensive. Security is not always the most popular department in a company. There are those that will do what they can to cause grief or drama. The best approach to take when you have failed to achieve improvement in an area is to conduct a transparent review of everything that occurred to find the root cause or causes. This is not an effort to make excuses, but something happened to derail the improvement project, and you need to understand what. Once you have your answer, you need to openly share it and own it. You also need to have a plan for addressing the roadblocks and taking another crack at it. If it was a resource issue, you should have the metrics and supporting data needed to submit a business case to close the gap. It could be a technical issue or lack of engagement from another department or perhaps your staff is overtasked. You data should back up your conclusions.

Your detractors may want to take the opportunity to make the SOC look bad for whatever reason, but if you approach it right, you may in fact be able to use the initial failure as a way to get a business case approved for additional resources. Of course, if you take this approach and get whatever resource you asked for, you then need to deliver. If you feel you've exhausted even those type of opportunities, make sure that you have your business case ready with up-to-date information that justifies your existence and clearly proves that you are the lowest cost provider, because sooner or later, someone will come asking.

HISTORICAL LESSONS

Morale is an important part of any department. You've built trust with the rest of the company, but you need to make sure that you also have built in that trust and respect at the SOC department level. There is a fine line between working effectively and overworking. At one company, we had a couple of rough months where several changes were occurring across the company and employees would call our SOC to take out their frustrations due to various reasons that sometimes was not even security-related on the operators who would be left angry, demoralized, and frustrated. We had a team meeting and as management said all the right things, but it became clear that while temporary, it was going to suck for the SCOs a while at least until the corporation's morale improved. We decided to bring in a body opponent bag (BOB) as our anger management specialist. We went out and purchased a BOB, which is a punching bag in the shape of a man's torso and head on a stand filled with water to keep it from falling over. When a particularly nasty call came in, the operators would handle it as best they could, making sure to remain professional. Then they would get up from their workstation, declare that they were going to have a counseling session with BOB, then walk over and give BOB a good solid punch or two or three or four to relieve their frustration. BOB got a lot of use in the first month and then less over time, but the gesture was appreciated for much longer and it was a constant reminder that we really did get what we were asking them to do and that at times it just plain sucked. Sometimes they will need to vent and you will need to listen. Being a security console operator is not an easy job at times. Remember that.

So, the moral of the story is, take care of your SOC staff because they are the sole reason that your SOC will succeed or fail. Take care of your people. Don't allow energy vampires and negative personalities to destroy the team morale of your SOC. Keep those post orders, and procedures up to date because your staff will rely on those to do the job. Provide them with the tools and training they need to complete their mission with each shift they work. Train them constantly, challenge them regularly, counsel them as needed, treat them kindly daily, give them opportunities to grow professionally, and remember to reward them when they are deserving because you are their leader. Remember to thank them for all their hard work and dedication on a regular basis. If you do all of that for your staff, your SOC will be a companywide success and a continuing integral part of the fabric of your organization that management will be proud of.

The authors of this book hope you have learned some valuable lessons or gained some good ideas or tips from this writing that you will be able to incorporate into your existing or future SOC. We ask that if you learn some new ideas along your SOC journey, please share them with us at securityopsctr@charter.net and your peers in the security industry to make as all better within our profession. We wish you and your SOC staff nothing but the best.

Index

Printed in the United States
By Bookmasters